Prairie Farmer.

POULTRY
C·O·O·K·B·O·O·K

MITZI AYALA

Cover photograph by Rural American Graphics.
Original needlepoint design created by Joy Kidney, West Des Moines, Iowa.

Cover design: Geri Wolfe

ISBN 0-87069-457-X

Library of Congress Catalog
Card Number 85-051023

10 9 8 7 6 5 4 3 2 1

Published by

Wallace-Homestead Book Company
580 Waters Edge
Lombard, Illinois 60148

This book is lovingly dedicated to the best grandparents Jose and Carlos could ever have, George and Grace Tooby.

Contents

Acknowledgments

The real authors of this book are the farm wives and the home economists who for 140 years have recorded and shared their favorite, most useful recipes. But there are other people who deserve credit as well. Bill Topaz and Steve Joss realized what a treasure trove of recipes lay hidden in the archives of Wallace-Homestead press. Carol Ford is responsible for the organization of this book and together with Nancy Ehrke, for the selection of the historical interest items you'll find as sidebars to the recipes.

Fred Kline from the Capitol News Service graciously permitted the use of some of the material from my newspaper column, *From the Farmer to You.*

These are the people who deserve credit. Now, how about a case in which credit is absolutely *not* deserved? It's a strange case, one in which events of more than a century ago reach across time and touch our lives today.

The creature that doesn't deserve any credit at all for the production of this book is—Mrs. Leary's cow.

When she kicked over the kerosene lantern back in 1871, the resulting fire reached the archives of Wallace-Homestead Press and destroyed several issues of the *Prairie Farmer, The Wisconsin Agriculturalist,* and *Wallaces Farmer.* Who knows what recipes were lost, ones that might have ended up being favorites for your family?

It's true that Mrs. Leary's cow caused us to lose a few recipes, but I think you'll find the remaining ones so delightful and so abundant that we can afford to forgive the cow.

Introduction

Tonight as you're making dinner, pause for a moment and think how easy cooking is today compared to what our great-grandmothers had to go through to put a meal on the table. A typical *Prairie Farmer* recipe from 1902 begins by directing the cook to:

"Singe (the bird) over a burning newspaper on a hot stove."

Probably in all of history, people have never had an easier, faster time cooking than today. Reading some of the recipes and tips that our grandmothers followed can give us a renewed appreciation of just how good we have it today.

Even though today's recipes may be faster and easier than those of the past, our grandmothers still have a lot to offer us in the way of unusual, delectable, and imaginative cooking. This book is a respectful tribute to a heritage of great cooking that we mustn't lose—and a celebration of the bounty and convenience we enjoy today. In offering you this book, we hope to share with you our choices of the best from both the past and the present.

In chapter one you'll discover that just a couple of generations ago, chicken was such a rare and expensive treat that only the rich could afford it and *Prairie Farmer* recipes from back then tell how to make "mock chicken" from the cheaper veal or beef. You probably don't need to know how to make mock chicken—although we hope you'll enjoy reading about it—but you may find a new family favorite from such recipes as the decorative Drumstick Prune Crown, or the homey 1902 Chicken Pie, or today's modern slow-cooked California Chicken.

Midwestern wives are thrifty, so over the years *Prairie Farmer's* cooks have developed some really special ways of using leftovers. Try Volcanos (it's chicken in a pyramidlike "volcano" of biscuit dough) when you want to make a special dinner from leftovers. Or how about Quick, Slick Casserole when you've had a busy day?

Chapter two will let you in on a secret that the soup manufacturers and the baby food makers know. Once you know it, you can both save money and get better flavor when serving chicken. It has to do with flavor chemistry, but it's really simple and you don't have to be a chemist to utilize it. In fact, if you learn one single word, you can take advantage of this money-saving tip.

You'll also find out about the Twiggies and the Marilyn Monroes of the chicken world. Some of our favorites from this chapter are Rissoles, Down South Stew, or Chicken in Paprika Cream.

We think you'll enjoy chapter three on preparation of turkey and other turkey secrets. During the 140 years that *Prairie Farmer* has been published, cooks have wondered what to do with turkey leftovers. This chapter gives you some of their answers. How about Turkey Swirls with Cranberry Sauce or Topsy Turvey Turkey—in this case the turkey is the stuffing for the casserole.

There are recipes for wild duck in chapter four that are superb. You'll also learn why you'll never find duck in the supermarket. You can find something quite similar, and it tastes about the same, and the name is almost the same . . . but it's *not* duck.

Chapter five covers The Long Form and The Short Form—but it's not about taxes. It's about the absolute best way to cook your goose. If there are any leftovers, try a Goose Puff.

You'll learn how pheasants in the future may be more economical and available than ever before because of better wildlife utilization. Chapter six offers tips from a lady who raises tens of thousands of pheasants every year. She'll tell you how to age them for the best flavor and how to freeze them so that they'll maintain quality. You'll also discover new and different recipes such as Barbecued Pheasant Teriyaki, Pheasant Baked in Beer, Deep Fried Pheasant Four Ways, or Braised Pheasant Kiev.

As for chapter seven, when you've read it, you'll know something that great-grandmother didn't know, something so valuable that you probably couldn't put a price on it. In the past, when we didn't know all that we know today about food safety and bacteria, many's the family that had tummy aches or cramps the next day, or just felt under the weather and never knew why. This chapter gives tips on how to keep unwanted salmonella and staphlococci bacteria at bay. Stuffing recipes that you'll find include: Rice and Wheat Stuffing, Peanut Stuffing, Easy Mincemeat Stuffing, a delectable Cranberry Bread Stuffing, and Elegant Oyster-Rice Stuffing.

Enjoy the cookbook. We wrote it, quite frankly, to be read as well as used. Bon Appetit!

1

Herbert Hoover Would Have Been Surprised

Napoleon's cook once bet that he could prepare chicken a different way for each day of the year. When you see the chicken recipes that follow, you'll see why he easily won that bet. From Party Sandwich Pinwheels to Brunswick Stew to Creole Chicken Shortcakes, farm cooks have developed an impressive number of approaches to cooking this adaptable bird.

Chicken has always been a versatile food, but it's only recently that it has become an affordable food. In 1928 when Herbert Hoover used "a chicken in every pot" as his campaign slogan, people thought it was the equivalent to promising them pie in the sky.

Back in 1928 when Hoover made that promise, chicken was a rich man's food. Having chicken for Sunday dinner was a sign of affluence, and for the average workingman's family, chicken was a rare and special treat. Even for many farm families, chicken was something of a luxury. *Prairie Farmer* recipes from back then often explain how to make "mock" chicken from veal or pork, since many couldn't afford the real thing.

Hoover's promise sounded far-fetched to most people, but not to Mrs. Wilmer Steele, a former egg producer from Sussex County, Maryland. She was the pioneer of today's broiler industry who got into this hitherto unknown

business by a fortunate accident—an accident from five years before that was destined to help make Hoover's promise of a chicken in every pot come true.

In 1923 when Mrs. Steele ordered 50 baby chicks to upgrade her laying flock, someone made a mistake with her order and sent 500 baby chicks instead. Mrs. Steele must have looked at those 500 chicks and known immediately that when they were grown, they'd lay more eggs than all of Sussex County could consume. How could she possibly sell *that* many eggs? How could she afford to feed that many chickens? To cut her losses, she decided to sell the birds for meat while they were still only a few months old and hadn't cost her too much in feed.

Selling young birds—eventually known as "broilers" or "fryers"—turned out to be a lucrative business. Consumers liked the tender meat from the young birds, and Mrs. Steele discovered that raising chickens entirely for meat, and not just as an adjunct to producing eggs, was a very efficient way of doing business. Specializing in producing meat rather than eggs meant that she could take advantage of mass-production techniques just as Henry Ford was doing with his automobiles. And just as Henry Ford helped make the automobile affordable, so Mrs. Steele helped make chicken affordable.

Mrs. Steele's enterprise was almost a backyard operation compared to the 150,000 birds that a typical poultryman raises today. The mass production was pioneered by Mrs. Steele, but there's also another factor—today's poultryman or woman is more efficient than Mrs. Steele could have imagined.

In 1928, a farmer would need to feed the chicks for at least 16 weeks to reach a market size of only three pounds. Today he or she grows birds that reach market size of four pounds in less than seven weeks.

Not only that, the grower does it using half the amount of feed. Today, two pounds of feed can yield one pound of chicken. In Mrs. Steele's time it took four pounds to produce a pound of bird.

Today's chickens are a bargain for us because they are bigger, grow faster, and utilize feed more efficiently than ever before. But what about taste? Did great-grandmother's birds have a better flavor? The U.S. Department of Agriculture wondered the same thing and arranged a clever test to find out. They asked a panel of experienced taste-testers to compare the flavor of modern chickens with birds from 1930s breeding stock. For a further refinement of the test, the 1930s birds were raised on 1930s rations.

When the panelists tried broilers from each flock, they couldn't detect any difference in flavor between the modern ones and the old-fashioned ones.

Chicken costs less today, and it still tastes good, but there are some other changes that have taken place since our grandmothers and great-grandmothers were first using these recipes. Today we have a lot more scientific knowledge of what we're doing when we cook poultry.

Today we understand why chicken is tough if it's either undercooked or overcooked, and we know more about how to get it just right. The thing to aim for when cooking chicken is to tenderize it by getting enough heat to break down the proteins and connective tissue in the muscles to make them tender. The thing to avoid is toughening the bird by cooking it beyond this point. Cooking chicken longer makes the protein in the muscle fibers become "denatured" and coagulated. In other words, as the meat loses more and more water, the proteins clump together and that means toughened chicken.

How do you tell when the meat has been cooked just long enough? For roast chicken, use a thermometer and cook until internal temperature reaches between 180 and 185 degrees.

If you don't have a thermometer, try these tests for doneness:
- The meat should be tender when pierced with a fork.
- The juices should be clear rather than dark or pinkish.
- The drumstick should feel soft when pressed between thumb and forefinger.
- The drumstick should move freely when lifted or twisted.

These tests will tell you if your fried chicken is done:
- It should be tender when pierced with a fork.
- The drumstick meat should be soft enough so that it can be easily dislodged from the bone.

By the way, there is no such thing as "medium" or "rare" chicken. It should always be cooked until it's fork tender.

Enjoy the recipes that follow and, as you do, think how surprised Napoleon's cook and President Hoover would be if they could see you cooking with chicken so often and in so many ways. "A chicken in every pot" isn't even worth crowing about today. But the variety, economy, and flavor is.

Menu for an Outdoor Barbecue

Barbecued Chicken*
Potato Salad*
Carrot and Celery Sticks
Hot French Bread* and Butter
Watermelon Slices
Oatmeal Cookies
Milk
Iced Tea or Coffee
*Recipe included

There's something about the aroma of chicken sizzling on the grill that can't be matched in modern kitchens. Maybe it's because today's kitchens aren't as big. And outdoors, the whole family, plus friends, can enjoy the mouth-watering anticipation of good things cooking.

Here are a couple of good tricks for outdoor dining. Make the potato salad at least six to eight hours in advance, so the seasonings have a chance to meld with the potatoes. And remember, a small paint brush is the handiest tool for generously swabbing the barbecue sauce on chicken pieces or on spareribs and hamburgers over an open fire.

Barbecued Chicken

broiler/chickens, cut into serving
  pieces, as needed
Barbecue Sauce:
¼ cup molasses
¼ cup vinegar or lemon juice
¼ cup prepared mustard
2 T. Worcestershire sauce
2 tsp. hot pepper sauce

Combine all ingredients. Makes ¾ cup, or enough sauce for three chickens (or 12 to 18 hamburgers).

Prepare charcoal grill. When coals are glowing, arrange three broiler/fryer chicken halves, cut side down, on greased grill or in a folding wire broiler. Grill slowly about 45 to 50 minutes or until tender, turning with tongs and basting often with Barbecue Sauce.
July 23, 1977

Potato Salad

3 pounds potatoes, with skins
1 small onion, chopped
2 cups celery, diced
1 green pepper, chopped
6 to 8 radishes, sliced
2 tsp. salt
1 cup mayonnaise
2 T. prepared mustard
2 T. vinegar
½ tsp. hot red pepper sauce
salad greens, as needed for garnish
tomato wedges, as needed for garnish

Cook potatoes until tender. Peel and dice. Add onion, celery, green pepper, and radishes. Sprinkle with salt. Mix together mayonnaise, mustard, vinegar, and pepper sauce. Add to potato mixture. Mix lightly with a fork, being careful not to break potatoes. Chill.

To serve, garnish with salad greens and tomatoes.
12 servings
July 23, 1977

Hot French Bread

2 long loaves or 2 round loaves
  French bread
softened butter, as needed

Slice bread in thick slices, almost through to the bottom. Butter each slice. Wrap each loaf with heavy-duty foil. Heat on the grill along with the chicken for about 30 minutes.
12 servings

10

Appetizers

Chicken Cocktail

¾ cup chili sauce
1 T. lemon juice
1½ tsp. prepared horseradish
5 or 6 drops Tabasco®
lettuce, as needed
¾ cup diced celery
1½ cups cooked chicken, diced
6 lemon wedges

Combine chili sauce, lemon juice, horseradish, and Tabasco®; chill well. Line individual cocktail cups with lettuce. Place celery on lettuce and top with chicken. Pour cocktail sauce over and serve with lemon wedges.
6 servings
September 16, 1961

Chicken Liver Pinwheel Sandwiches

Filling:
1 T. onion, finely minced
2 T. butter
½ cup chopped chicken livers
¼ cup ham, minced
pinch of salt
1 egg, slightly beaten

Saute onion in butter for about two minutes. Add chicken livers and cook for seven or eight minutes over medium heat, stirring often. Add ham and salt. Cook about five minutes longer. Stir in egg and cook only until thickened.
To assemble:
several slices white or whole wheat bread*
chicken liver spread
butter, as needed

Cut crusts from the bread, and roll each slice slightly with a rolling pin to flatten. Spread with butter and liver spread and roll up as for a jelly roll.

Chill in the refrigerator for at least an hour. If rushed, store in freezer for a few minutes.

To serve, unwrap and cut each roll in thirds.

*You can use slices from sliced bread, or you can use the large slices made from a loaf of unsliced bread that has been cut horizontally.
April 18, 1959

Chicken Liver Pâté

3 T. butter
⅔ cup onion, finely chopped
⅓ cup celery, finely chopped
1 tsp. garlic salt
¼ tsp. pepper
¼ tsp. basil
¼ tsp. oregano
8 ounces broiler-fryer chicken livers
2 T. tomato sauce
4 ounces mozzarella cheese, finely grated
celery stalks, as needed

Melt butter in skillet. Saute onion and chopped celery in butter. Stir in garlic salt, pepper, basil, and oregano. Add chicken livers and saute until evenly brown on all sides. Pour liver-onion mixture into blender; add tomato sauce. Blend on low speed for 30 seconds (do not puree). Refrigerate liver mixture.

When chilled, add grated cheese; stir well until all ingredients are completely mixed. Stuff celery stalks with pâté. Refrigerate until ready to serve.
2 cups pâté
December, 1977

Rumaki

½ pound bacon
1 8-ounce can water chestnuts
½ pound chicken livers, cut into
    ¾-inch pieces
fat for frying, as needed

Drain water chestnuts and dry. Cut in half crosswise. Cut bacon slices in half crosswise. Place a chicken liver and a chestnut half on each piece of bacon. Roll up and fasten with a toothpick. Fry rolls until golden brown. Drain.
Serve hot as an appetizer.
February 4, 1961

This recipe from 1916 makes an attractive—and surprising—appetizer when set on crisp lettuce leaves.

Eggs Stuffed with Chicken

Boil the eggs until hard, then cut in halves with a sharp knife, and remove the yolks. Mince these with some finely cut chicken, adding a little butter, a few grains of salt and pepper, and a grating of nutmeg. Refill the whites with this mixture, press the halves well together, using a little raw white of egg to make the joining smooth, and arrange on serving dish.
September 28, 1916

Cheese Garnishes

Cheese goes well with soup, in it, or on it. . . . Sprinkle hot soups with grated parmesan. . . . Spread cream cheese on rounds of melba toast and float in soup. . . . Serve the family's favorite cheese with crackers on the side. . . . Cut outlines of dolls, animals, or stars in slices of processed cheese and slip gently on children's hot soup.
Prairie Farmer, January 3, 1956

Soups

Mock Chicken Stew

3 medium-sized onions
3 T. fat
2 cups diced raw potatoes
2 cups kidney beans
3 cups water
1 cup canned tuna or white-fleshed fish

Melt fat, add onion, sliced, and cook until slightly brown; add beans, which have been previously boiled, potatoes and water. Cover and cook slowly until potatoes are tender; season with salt and pepper, add fish, and let stand over fire until thoroughly heated.
January 31, 1918

Chicken Chowder

2 ounces salt pork, finely diced or 4
    T. chicken fat
1 cup cooked chicken, diced
2 to 4 T. onion, finely chopped
2½ cups potatoes, diced to ½-inch
    squares
1 cup celery, diced into ½-inch pieces
2 cups chicken stock
1 20-ounce can kernel corn
1 tall can evaporated milk
¼ tsp. paprika
¼ tsp. ginger
1 tsp. salt
¼ tsp. pepper
2 T. parsley, chopped
crackers, rolls, or toast, as desired

Cook salt pork in saucepan over low heat until lightly browned. Add chicken and onion and cook until onion is soft but not browned. Add potatoes, celery, and chicken stock. Simmer vegetables until tender. Add corn, milk, paprika, ginger, salt, pepper, and parsley. Heat thoroughly, stirring occasionally. Season to taste with additional salt and pepper, if desired.
    Serve very hot with crackers, hard rolls, or toast.
6 servings
April 1, 1944

Chicken Egg Drop Soup

6 cups chicken broth
2 T. cornstarch
2 T. cold water
1 T. soy sauce
½ tsp. sugar
2 eggs, slightly beaten
2 green onions, chopped (including
    green tops)
salt and pepper, to taste

In a large saucepan, heat broth to boiling. Blend cornstarch and water to make a smooth paste; stir in soy sauce and sugar. Slowly stir into broth; bring to boil and simmer until clear, stirring constantly. Remove from heat. Gradually add eggs, stirring until eggs separate into shreds. Add green onions, salt, and pepper.
4 servings
January 14, 1974

Chicken Gumbo

½ cup canned tomatoes
½ cup celery, thinly sliced
½ green pepper, thinly sliced
½ cup onion, thinly sliced
½ T. parsley, finely chopped
4 chicken bouillon cubes
4 cups chicken broth
2 cups cooked chicken, diced
1 (10-ounce) package okra
½ cup cooked rice
½ cup cooked corn

Add tomatoes, celery, green pepper, onion, parsley, and bouillon cubes to broth. Simmer 20 minutes, or until vegetables are tender. Add chicken and okra and cook five minutes longer. Add rice and corn and heat to serving temperature.
6 servings
January 14, 1974

Curried Chicken Stew

1 broiler-fryer chicken, cut into
    serving pieces
¼ cup all-purpose flour
1 tsp. salt
¼ tsp. pepper
¼ cup butter or margarine
½ cup celery, chopped
¼ cup onion, chopped
2 T. parsley, chopped
1 clove garlic, minced
1½ tsp. curry powder
½ tsp. dried leaf thyme
1 can (1 pound) tomatoes
3 T. raisins

Coat chicken pieces with mixture of flour, salt, and pepper. Brown in butter in skillet. Add celery, onion, parsley, garlic, curry powder, and thyme to skillet; cook until celery and onion are tender. Add tomatoes; bring to a boil. Cover and simmer 15 minutes. Uncover; add raisins and simmer 10 to 15 minutes longer, until chicken is tender.
   If desired, serve with rice.
4 servings
November 9, 1974

Roquefort Chicken Soup

2½ cups chicken broth
½ cup cream
2½ T. all-purpose flour
3 T. chicken broth
2 to 3 T. Roquefort cheese, crumbled

Combine two and one-half cups broth and cream. Blend flour and three tablespoons broth to a smooth paste. Add to broth and simmer until thick. Add Roquefort cheese and simmer for a few minutes longer.
3 servings
March 18, 1961

By all accounts, every place named Brunswick, from Canada to the Carolinas, has tried to claim Brunswick Stew as its own. There have also been as many arguments about what precisely went into the original pot, and what should go in now. All in all, Brunswick County in Virginia has the best claim to being the birthplace of this popular dish that in its heyday was served at Virginia's tobacco-curings and public gatherings. The story goes that a hunting party in Brunswick County, well provisioned with tomatoes, onions, corn, cabbage, beans, and bacon, left one man behind to mind the commisary and have dinner ready at day's end. Disgruntled, he shot a squirrel, the only thing he could find within range of the camp, and threw it into the pot along with the vegetables. When it was served, everybody agreed that squirrel was what made the stew just right. Squirrels gradually disappeared from the recipes for Brunswick Stew and chicken is now accepted as its major ingredient.

And if you have the time, remember it is a rule in some tidewater homes never to eat Brunswick Stew the same day it is made since its flavor improves if it is left to stand overnight and reheated before serving.

New Brunswick Stew

*1 3-pound chicken, cut in serving
  pieces
1 quart water
1 large onion, sliced
1 cup okra, cut (or 10-ounce
  package frozen), if desired
2 cups tomatoes (or 1-pound can)
1 cup lima beans (or 10-ounce
  package frozen)
2 medium potatoes, diced
2 cups corn cut from the cob (or
  1-pound can or 10-ounce package
  frozen)
1½ tsp. salt
½ tsp. pepper
1½ tsp. sugar*

Simmer chicken in water until meat can be easily removed from the bones. Remove meat from broth. Add raw vegetables and simmer, uncovered, until beans and potatoes are tender. Stir occasionally to prevent scorching.

Meanwhile, bone and dice chicken meat. Add chicken, remaining vegetables, salt, pepper, and sugar. Simmer for 15 minutes. If canned vegetables are used, include juices and reduce water by one cup.
8 servings
September 20, 1975

When you are looking for a good and hearty soup that doesn't take long to prepare, try this one:

Potato Chicken Soup

6 slices bacon, cut in 1-inch pieces
⅔ cup onion, chopped (or frozen chives)
2 medium potatoes, peeled and diced
1 cup water
¾ tsp. salt
2 10½-ounce cans cream of chicken soup
2½ cups milk
2 T. parsley, chopped

In a large saucepan, cook bacon until crisp. Remove from pan and set aside. Pour off all but three tablespoons of fat. Add onions and cook slightly. Add potatoes, water, and salt. Cover and cook for 10 minutes, or until potatoes are tender. Mash slightly, if desired. Blend in undiluted soup and milk. Heat, but do not boil.

To serve, garnish with parsley and bacon.
4 to 6 servings
October 3, 1964

Corn and Chicken Chowder

2 T. butter
½ cup onion, finely chopped
1 cup uncooked potato, finely diced
1 cup chicken broth
1 cup cooked chicken, finely chopped
2 cups cream-style corn
salt and pepper, to taste
2 T. parsley, minced

Melt butter in saucepan, add onion, and cook and stir until yellow. Add potato and chicken broth, cover and cook until potato is tender. Add chicken, corn, salt, and pepper and heat until boiling. Add additional seasoning, if necessary.

Serve in warm bowls. Garnish with parsley.
4 servings
January 6, 1962

Easy Chicken Stew

1 2½- to 3-pound chicken, cut into serving pieces
⅓ cup all-purpose flour
¼ cup shortening
1 cup water
4 medium carrots, peeled and quartered
4 medium potatoes, peeled and quartered
4 medium onions, peeled and quartered
1 tsp. salt
2 cans (10½ ounces) cream of chicken soup
1 package (10 ounces) frozen peas, thawed enough to separate

Shake chicken in flour in a paper bag. Brown chicken in hot shortening in a five-quart Dutch oven over medium heat. Drain. Add water, carrots, potatoes, onions, and salt. Pour soup over chicken and vegetables. Cover. Simmer over low heat one hour and 15 minutes, or until chicken and vegetables are tender. Add peas. Simmer 15 minutes more.
4 to 6 servings
April 22, 1958

Salads

Chicken-Grape Salad

2 cups cooked chicken, cubed
1 cup seedless grapes
⅓ cup slivered toasted almonds
⅓ cup pimiento, cut in strips
sharp mayonnaise, as needed
salad greens, as needed

Combine chicken, grapes, almonds, and pimiento. Moisten with mayonnaise. Chill.

To serve, arrange lettuce leaves on six luncheon plates, and pile chicken mixture in center.
6 servings
July 5, 1958

Hot Chicken Salad

2 cups cooked chicken, chopped
2 cups celery, chopped
½ cup blanched almonds, chopped
2 T. pimiento, chopped
½ tsp. salt
2 T. lemon juice
½ cup mayonnaise
2 cups potato chips, crushed
½ cup Swiss cheese, grated

Blend chicken, celery, almonds, pimiento, salt, lemon juice, and mayonnaise. Put alternate layers of the chicken mixture and potato chips in a buttered 1½-quart casserole. Top with a layer of potato chips and the cheese.

Bake in a 350 degree oven for 20 to 25 minutes, or until cheese is melted.
6 to 8 servings
February 6, 1965

Chicken-Ham Mold

2 envelopes gelatin
1 cup cold water
2 cans condensed tomato soup
2 T. lemon juice
1 T. prepared mustard
1 tsp. horseradish
1 T. Worcestershire sauce
1 tsp. thyme
1 cup ham, chopped
1 cup cooked chicken, cubed

Soften gelatin in water. Heat soup, add gelatin, and stir until dissolved. Stir in lemon juice, mustard, horseradish, Worcestershire sauce, and thyme. Pour into oiled mold, such as a loaf pan. Chill until partially set, then fold in ham and chicken. Chill until set.

To serve, unmold on platter.
6 servings
March 2, 1963

Chicken Salad

3 cups cooked chicken, chopped
½ cup French dressing
1 cup mayonnaise or your favorite
  cooked salad dressing
¼ cup whipped cream
4 hard-cooked eggs
½ cup sweet pickle, chopped
2 cups celery, diced
salt, to taste
salad greens, as needed

Marinate chicken in French dressing for about 30 minutes. Combine mayonnaise and whipped cream. Lightly toss with chicken, eggs, pickle, celery, and salt.

To serve, divide evenly over salad greens.
4 to 6 servings
May 19, 1962

New Horizon Chicken Salad

1 T. orange peel, grated
2 oranges, peeled, cut in bite-size
   pieces
1½ cups cooked chicken, chopped
⅔ cup celery, chopped
½ cup toasted almonds, sliced
1 package (3 ounces) cream cheese,
   softened
2 to 3 T. mayonnaise or salad dressing
½ tsp. salt
⅛ tsp. pepper
4 lettuce cups

Combine all ingredients except lettuce. Spoon about one cup chicken mixture into each lettuce cup.

This mixture may also be used for sandwich filling.
4 servings
July 9, 1977

Chicken Almond Mousse Salad

1 package (3 ounces) lime flavored
   gelatin
1 T. (1 envelope) unflavored gelatin
1½ cups boiling water
1 cup chicken stock
3 cups cooked chicken, finely
   chopped
¾ cup celery, finely chopped
½ cup almonds, chopped
⅓ cup cucumber, finely chopped
   and drained
2 T. lemon juice
2 tsp. salt
1 cup whipping cream, whipped

In a bowl combine lime gelatin and unflavored gelatin; pour boiling water over gelatins, and stir until dissolved. Blend in chicken stock; chill until partially set. Add chicken, celery, almonds, cucumber, lemon juice, and salt. Fold in whipped cream. Turn into oiled salad mold. Chill until firm.

Dressing:

1 tsp. celery salt
1 tsp. lemon juice
1 cup sour cream

Blend salt and lemon juice into sour cream. Cover and chill.

To serve, unmold mousse onto serving plate; pour dressing over.
6 to 8 servings
June 11, 1966

Chicken-Lettuce Oriental

1 medium head iceberg lettuce,
   cored, rinsed, and drained
⅓ cup soy sauce
¼ cup white wine, or 3 T. lemon
   juice and 1 T. sugar
1 T. sugar
1 tsp. ground ginger
1 clove garlic, minced
1 frying chicken (2½ pounds), cut
   into serving pieces
¼ cup blanched whole almonds
2 T. oil
1 can (13½ ounces) pineapple chunks
1 T. cornstarch

Chill lettuce in plastic bag or lettuce "crisp-it." In shallow dish combine soy sauce, wine, sugar, ginger, and garlic. Place chicken in mixture and marinate one hour, turning and basting occasionally.

Place chicken in baking pan. Bake in 325 degree oven for one hour, basting twice with marinade. Brown almonds in oil in skillet. Remove and drain on paper towels. Add pineapple, not drained, to skillet. Heat. Add cornstarch to remaining marinade. Add to pineapple. Cook and stir until sauce comes to a boil and is thickened. Add chicken and almonds.

Cut lettuce crosswise into slices. Place lettuce cut side down on board and cut crosswise and lengthwise into bite-size chunks. Line platter with lettuce chunks. Spoon chicken and sauce over lettuce. Serve immediately.
4 servings
January 4, 1958

Chicken Cashew Salad

4 cups cooked chicken, diced
1 cup celery, thinly sliced
¼ cup salted cashews, chopped
¼ cup mayonnaise
2 T. sour cream
2 T. bottled horseradish sauce dressing
salad greens, as needed
paprika, as desired

Combine chicken, celery, and cashews in salad bowl. Blend together mayonnaise, sour cream, and horseradish dressing. Chill salad and dressing.

At serving time, mix dressing thoroughly into salad and serve on salad greens. Sprinkle with paprika.
4 to 5 servings
June 11, 1977

Polynesian Salad

½ cup sour cream
½ cup mayonnaise
½ tsp. curry powder
¼ tsp. ginger
salt and pepper, to taste
3 to 4 cups cooked chicken, cubed
20-ounce can pineapple chunks,
*   drained*
½ to ¾ cup slivered almonds or
*   diced macadamia nuts*
lettuce leaves, as needed

Combine the sour cream, mayonnaise, curry powder, and ginger; mix well. Add salt and pepper. Let stand 15 minutes or more. Combine chicken, pineapple chunks, and nuts. Mix lightly with the dressing until all pieces are coated.

Serve on lettuce leaves.
6 to 8 servings
June 13, 1970

Chicken and Rice Salad

2 T. corn oil
2 T. vinegar
2 T. onion, finely chopped
1½ tsp. salt
1 tsp. curry powder (optional)
pepper, to taste
1½ cups cooked rice
1½ cups cooked chicken, cubed
1 cup celery, chopped
2 T. green pepper, chopped
¾ cup mayonnaise
salad greens, as needed

Combine corn oil, vinegar, onion, salt, curry powder, and pepper. Add to rice. Toss lightly until seasonings are well mixed with rice. Place in refrigerator for about one hour.

Just before serving, add chicken, celery, green pepper, and mayonnaise and mix thoroughly. Serve on greens.
6 servings
June 17, 1967

Campers' Choice

6 cups water
1 T. seasoned chicken stock base
1 tsp. salt
3 cups medium noodles
3 cups cooked chicken, chopped
1 cup celery, thinly sliced
½ cup radishes, sliced
¼ cup green onion, sliced
1 cup sour cream
1 tsp. seasoned salt
¼ tsp. poultry seasoning

Bring water, stock base, and salt to a boil in a saucepan. Add noodles and cook according to package directions; rinse with cold water and drain. Combine chicken, celery, radishes, onion, and noodles in a large bowl. Mix sour cream, seasoned salt, and poultry seasoning; fold into chicken mixture. Chill.
8 cups
June 22, 1974

Molded Chicken a la King

Sometimes a bit of chicken is left over, and we wonder how to serve it. When brought to the table, it should be attractive, delicious, and nutritious. Here is one way to meet all three requirements:

2 T. butter
1 cup milk, scalded
⅓ cup hot chicken broth
¼ cup green pepper, chopped
¼ cup pimiento, chopped
1 cup cooked chicken, diced
½ cup mushrooms, sliced
1 T. unflavored gelatin
2 T. cold water
4 egg yolks
2 T. lemon juice
3 to 4 tomatoes, cut into wedges
2 T. parsley, chopped
3 to 4 hard-cooked eggs, sliced

Cook butter, milk, broth, green pepper, pimiento, chicken, and mushrooms in the top of a double boiler until the green pepper is tender. Soften gelatin in water. Beat egg yolks, and add lemon juice. Pour a little of the hot liquid over the yolks, stirring constantly, then stir yolks into chicken mixture. Cook over boiling water for five minutes, stirring constantly.

Remove from heat and stir into softened gelatin. Turn into an oiled mold and chill until firm.

To serve, unmold onto a serving platter and garnish with tomatoes, parsley, and eggs. Cut in half-inch slices.
8 servings
December 2, 1950

Chicken Mousse

1 envelope unflavored gelatin
1½ cups chicken broth, divided
1 T. onion juice
1¼ cups cooked chicken, diced
2 T. celery, chopped
1 T. stuffed olives, chopped
1 cup heavy cream, whipped
watercress, as needed
radish roses, if desired, for garnish

Sprinkle gelatin on one-half cup of the chicken broth to soften. Place over low heat and stir until gelatin is dissolved. Remove from heat and stir in remaining one cup chicken broth and onion juice. Chill mixture to unbeaten egg white consistency. Fold in chicken, celery, olives, and whipped cream. Turn into a four-cup oiled mold and chill until firm.

Unmold on serving plate and garnish with watercress and radish roses.
4 servings
May 7, 1966

Chicken Cranberry Salad

2 envelopes unflavored gelatin
¼ cup cold water
2 cans condensed cream of chicken
  soup
¼ cup mayonnaise
1 T. parsley, minced
1 can jellied cranberry sauce
1 envelope unflavored gelatin
¼ cup cold water

Soften two envelopes gelatin in water. Heat one-quarter can soup; add gelatin and dissolve. Stir dissolved gelatin into remaining soup; cool. Fold in mayonnaise and parsley. Pour soup mixture into one and one-half-quart oiled mold; chill until firm. Crush cranberry sauce with fork. Soften one envelope gelatin in cold water; set in pan of boiling water and stir until gelatin is dissolved. Combine gelatin and cranberry sauce; pour on top of firm chicken layer; continue to chill until cranberry layer is firm.

Unmold when ready to serve. Serve on greens or with garnish as desired.
6 servings
November 13, 1965

Here's a favorite regional recipe from the Midwest:

Baked Chicken Salad

2 cups cooked chicken, diced
1 T. onion, minced
2 cups celery, chopped
1 cup mayonnaise
3 T. lemon juice
½ cup slivered blanched almonds
  (2-ounce package)
¾ tsp. salt
⅛ tsp. pepper
½ cup sharp cheddar cheese, grated
1 cup seasoned croutons

Preheat oven to 425 degrees.

Lightly butter a one and one-half quart baking dish. Mix together chicken, onion, celery, mayonnaise, lemon juice, almonds, salt, and pepper and place in baking dish. Toss cheese and croutons together and sprinkle over top.

Bake in oven for 15 to 20 minutes.
4 to 6 servings
September 18, 1976

Sandwiches

Slick Chick Spread

1 cup chicken livers
½ medium onion, chopped
1 T. butter
2 hard-cooked eggs, finely chopped
1 T. mayonnaise
few drops lemon juice
salt and pepper, to taste

Saute chicken livers and onion in butter until livers are done and onion is transparent. Finely chop the mixture. Stir in eggs, mayonnaise, lemon juice, salt, and pepper. Chill.
1½ cups spread
August 7, 1965

Ham and Chicken Cheesewiches

¼ cup (½ stick) butter
¼ cup all-purpose flour
1 tsp. dry mustard
1½ cups milk
1 tsp. Worcestershire sauce
1½ cups cheddar cheese, shredded
1 cup cooked ham, diced
6 slices white chicken meat
6 slices toast

In a saucepan melt butter. Blend in flour and mustard. Gradually stir in milk and Worcestershire sauce; cook, stirring constantly until sauce is thickened. Add cheese, stirring until melted. Add ham and heat thoroughly. Put slices of chicken on toast. Serve topped with the hot cheese and ham sauce.
6 servings
August 7, 1965

Chicken or Turkey Turnabouts

6 to 8 enriched Vienna hard rolls
2 cups cooked chicken or turkey, chopped
⅔ cup celery, chopped
⅓ cup pitted ripe olives, chopped
1 T. onion, minced
¼ tsp. poultry seasoning
¼ tsp. pepper
1 can (10½ ounces) cream of chicken soup

Slice tops from rolls. Hollow out inside and reserve crumbs. Reserve shells. Combine two cups bread crumbs, chicken, celery, olives, onion, poultry seasoning, and pepper. Add soup and mix well. Fill reserved shells with chicken mixture.

Bake in 350 degree oven for 25 to 35 minutes, or until thoroughly heated.
6 to 8 servings
April 22, 1968

A hot and robust meal for a cold day or evening.

Chicken Sandwich a la Cheese

¼ cup butter
¼ cup all-purpose flour
1 tsp. salt
¼ tsp. mustard
dash of cayenne pepper
2 cups milk
2 cups (8 ounces) sharp cheese, chopped or grated
4 slices toast
2 cups cooked chicken, sliced
paprika, as desired
4 slices crisp bacon
8 slices tomato

Preheat oven to 450 degrees.

Melt butter over low heat. Add flour, salt, mustard, and cayenne pepper; blend thoroughly. Add milk, stirring constantly until thickened throughout. Add cheese and stir until blended.

Arrange toast on a heat-proof platter or in a shallow casserole; top with chicken. Cover with cheese sauce. Sprinkle with paprika.

Bake in oven (or under broiler) to heat until sauce is bubbly, about six to 10 minutes.

To serve, garnish with bacon and tomato. Serve immediately.

4 servings
January 4, 1958

Why make a lot of sandwiches for a crowd when you can make one big one? All of these party sandwiches look spectacular and are easy to assemble. Check through your recipe file of sandwich fillings. You may want to substitute some of your own favorites for the fillings suggested here. And remember, you can vary the garnishes according to fruits and vegetables in season. Or according to your personal taste.

Party Sandwich Pinwheel

9 slices white bread
9 slices whole wheat bread
½ cup tuna filling
½ cup egg salad filling
½ cup pineapple cream cheese filling
½ cup chicken salad filling
½ cup ham salad filling
cream cheese for frosting, as needed
garnishes, as desired (examples are
    shrimp, olives, pickled onions)

Trim crusts from bread. Alternate light and dark slices to make three sets of six slices each. Spread each of three bottom slices with tuna filling. Spread next set of slices with egg salad filling. Repeat with cream cheese, chicken, and ham fillings, then place remaining slice on top. Cut each stack diagonally in half.

Whip cream cheese until fluffy. Spread evenly on top and sides of each triangle. Arrange on plate like a pinwheel. Garnish as desired.

6 servings
April 13, 1968

And the following, although the original recipe doesn't include chicken, is a party sandwich using a round loaf of bread.

Luncheon Sandwich Loaf

1 round loaf Italian bread
2 8-ounce packages cream cheese
½ cup sour cream
2 T. chopped pitted black olives
2 T. chopped stuffed olives
1 pound cooked shrimp, chopped
    (leave a few whole for garnish)
2 T. fresh dill, finely chopped
mayonnaise, as needed
4 hard-cooked eggs, finely chopped
1 T. anchovy paste
½ cup watercress, chopped
cream or milk, as needed
dillweed sprays, if desired

Cut bread crosswise into four slices. Mash one package of the cream cheese; beat with sour cream until fluffy. Fold in black olives and stuffed olives; set aside. Mix shrimp, dill, and enough mayonnaise to make spreading consistency. Set aside. Combine eggs, anchovy paste, and watercress with enough mayonnaise to make spreading consistency.

Assemble loaf by spreading layers with the three mixtures and topping with the fourth slice. Whip remaining cream cheese with enough cream or milk to make it fluffy. Spread over loaf.

To serve, garnish with whole shrimp and dill weed sprays. Cut in wedges.

10 or 12 servings
April 13, 1968

And last, a way of making a party loaf using a loaf of unsliced bread:

Party Sandwich Loaf

1½-pound loaf unsliced bread
¼ cup butter, softened
1 can luncheon meat
2 T. pickle relish
2 T. mayonnaise
4 hard-cooked eggs, finely chopped
½ tsp. salt
⅛ tsp. pepper
3 T. green pepper, finely chopped
2 T. plus 2 tsp. onion, finely
* chopped*
¼ cup mayonnaise
½ cup ground cooked meat (or
* poultry) save ¼ cup of meat for*
* top layer*
2 T. ripe olives, finely chopped
¼ cup celery, minced
¼ cup mayonnaise
cream cheese, as needed
cream, as needed
olives, as needed for garnish

Trim crusts from bread. Cut crosswise into four slices; butter slices. Grind luncheon meat; mix with pickle relish and two tablespoons mayonnaise. Set aside. Combine egg, salt, pepper, green pepper, two teaspoons of the onion, and one-quarter cup mayonnaise; mix to spreading consistency. Set aside. Combine one-quarter cup of the meat, olives, celery, the remaining two tablespoons onion, and one-quarter cup mayonnaise.

Assemble layers with the three mixtures. Top with remaining ground cooked meat; wrap in waxed paper and chill for several hours or overnight. Cover with cream cheese softened with cream. Garnish with olives.
12 servings
April 13, 1968

Champion Two-Story Sandwich

First layer:
½ pound cooked chicken, sliced

Second layer:
4 hard-cooked eggs, chopped
2 T. celery, chopped
2 T. olives, chopped
1 T. sweet pickle, chopped
2 T. mayonnaise or salad dressing
2 tsp. prepared mustard
12 slices bread, buttered

Layer chicken on six slices of bread. Combine eggs, celery, olives, sweet pickle, mayonnaise, and mustard; place on chicken. Cover with remaining slices of bread.
6 sandwiches
September 5, 1970

Chicken-Ham Sandwich Filling

1 cup cooked chicken, diced
1 cup ham, finely chopped
¼ cup celery, chopped
¼ cup mayonnaise or salad dressing
3 T. prepared horseradish
1 tsp. lemon juice

Combine chicken, ham, celery, mayonnaise, horseradish, and lemon juice.
Makes 2 cups, or enough for 10 sandwiches
September 5, 1970

Chicken Waldorf Sandwich

1 cup cooked chicken, diced
½ cup celery, chopped
½ cup apple, chopped
¼ cup nuts, chopped
3 T. salad dressing or mayonnaise
12 slices bread

Combine chicken, celery, apple, nuts, and salad dressing. Spread on six slices of bread, and top with remaining slices.
6 sandwiches
September 5, 1970

A main-dish hot sandwich.

Chicken Rabbit Sandwich

2 T. butter
2 T. all-purpose flour
1 cup milk
½ pound American cheese
½ tsp. prepared mustard
1 tsp. Worcestershire sauce
salt, to taste
6 slices crisp toast
cooked chicken, thickly sliced, as
*   needed*
paprika, as desired

Melt butter in a saucepan, add flour, and blend. Add milk and cook, stirring constantly, until the sauce is smooth and thickened. Add cheese, mustard, Worcestershire, and salt; stir over low heat only until cheese is melted.

Arrange toast in individual shirred egg dishes, or one shallow baking pan; top with chicken, cover with cheese sauce, and sprinkle lightly with paprika.

Place under moderate broiler heat only until cheese sauce begins to brown lightly. Serve at once.
6 servings
March 17, 1962

A special sandwich.

Chicken Blackstone

½ cup butter
½ cup all-purpose flour
¼ tsp. salt
1 cup chicken stock
1 cup evaporated milk
2 cups cooked chicken, diced
12 French toast slices

Melt butter in top of a double boiler; blend in flour and salt. Combine stock with evaporated milk. Add to flour mixture and cook over low heat, stirring constantly until thickened. Add chicken; cook over hot water 10 minutes.

Place half of the slices of French toast in the bottom of a shallow baking dish, add chicken mixture, and top with remaining slices of French toast.

Bake in 350 degree oven for 15 minutes.
6 servings
May 2, 1959

A change of pace for the lunchbox.

Chicken-Swiss Cheese Sandwich Filling

1 cup cooked chicken, chopped
½ cup Swiss cheese, grated
2 T. green pepper, chopped
½ tsp. celery seeds
½ cup mayonnaise or salad dressing

Combine chicken, cheese, green pepper, celery seeds, and mayonnaise.
1½ cups, or enough for six sandwiches
September 17, 1960

Chicken Salad Spread

½ cup mayonnaise or salad dressing
1 dill pickle
1 stalk celery, cut into 2-inch pieces
¼ small onion
1 green pepper, sliced
¼ tsp. salt
⅛ tsp. pepper
2 hard-cooked eggs
1½ cups cooked chicken, diced

Put mayonnaise or salad dressing, pickle, celery, onion, green pepper, salt, and pepper into a blender container. Cover and "mix" about 20 seconds. Remove center cap, add eggs and chicken, and replace cover. Turn on and off at "chop" until chopped.
2 cups
May 25, 1974

Barbecued Chicken Sandwich

¾ cup water
½ cup catsup
¼ cup vinegar
2 T. dark brown sugar
1 tsp. instant minced onion
1 tsp. dry mustard
dash of Tabasco®
1 cup cooked chicken, diced
¼ cup green pepper, chopped
6 hamburger buns, toasted
butter, softened, as needed

Combine water, catsup, vinegar, sugar, onion, mustard, and Tabasco® in a small saucepan. Bring to a boil, reduce heat, and simmer 30 minutes. Add more water if necessary, to thin sauce to desired consistency. Stir in chicken and green pepper. Heat to serving temperature.

To serve, spread buns with butter. Spoon chicken mixture onto bottom halves, then close sandwiches. Serve hot.
6 servings
October 3, 1964

Chutney Chicken Sandwiches

1 can (20 ounces) pineapple chunks
2 T. instant minced onion
2 cups cooked chicken, diced
1 cup cucumbers, chunked
½ cup salted cashews, chopped
1 cup mayonnaise
2 T. chutney
1 tsp. seasoned salt
Crisp lettuce leaves, as needed
8 slices dark bread, buttered

Drain pineapple well, reserving 3 tablespoons juice. Combine onion and pineapple juice, allowing mixture to stand 10 minutes until moisture is absorbed. Meanwhile, combine chicken, cucumber, cashews, and pineapple in a large bowl. Combine mayonnaise, chutney, and seasoned salt. Add onions, blending well. Pour over chicken mixture.

Arrange lettuce leaves on buttered bread. Spoon chicken mixture onto lettuce.
8 servings
August 28, 1971

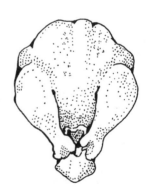

Main-Dish Recipes

To brighten up a meal and liven up appetites, add one of the following garnishes along with a few sprigs of parsley:

- A ring of sliced pineapple topped with a crabapple
- Orange or lemon cups filled with whole cranberry sauce
- Spiced peaches decorated with whole cloves or cream cheese
- Pear or peach halves filled with tangy jelly
- Small molds of jellied salad

Chicken a la Turque with Rice

Singe a roasting chicken of about three pounds, dry inside and out with a towel; cut in four pieces and place in a saucepan with one tablespoonful of melted butter, one of chopped white onion, and half a one of chopped green pepper. Brown slightly all around for ten minutes, then add one quart of good broth and three tablespoonfuls of canned tomatoes. Season with one teaspoonful of salt, one small bunch of celery, two cloves and one small bay leaf. Dilute in a little water one saltspoonful of saffron and pour over chicken. Add half a pint of uncooked rice well washed, and finish with two tablespoonfuls of fresh-grated cheese. Cook in a covered sauce pan for one hour. Turn over the pieces of chicken twice during the cooking, without disturbing the rice, so that each grain may be kept whole. Serve on a hot platter. Place the rice in the center in cone shape, the four quarters of chicken at the corners, and a few green pepper strips here and there.
October 5, 1905

Panned Spring Chicken

An appetizing way to serve chicken is to first split the chicken down the back, put in a dripping pan, cover with bits of butter and set in the oven. When partly done take out, season with salt, pepper and more butter and return to the oven to brown. When done, remove to hot platter and make gravy by adding hot water to butter and juices in pan. Thicken if desired. Serve hot.
July 13, 1905

Baked Chicken with Sweet Cream

Cut chicken in two lengthwise, place halves in a dripping pan and cover each half with sweet cream; season with salt, pepper and butter; set in oven; by the time the cream is almost cooked away the chicken will be done; have just cream enough left to pour over mashed potatoes as gravy.
August 1, 1901

Chicken Baked in Cream

Clean and cut up a spring chicken. Season with salt and pepper, dredge with flour, and place in a baking pan. Cover and cook till done, basting with a cupful of cream and half a cupful of melted butter, mixed. This is a southern recipe.
September 21, 1905

Add half a teaspoon each of poultry seasoning and caraway seed in the crust the next time you make a chicken or poultry pie. This gives a nice blend of flavors in the usual rolled crust.
Wisconsin Agriculturist And Farmer, September 20, 1958

Creole Chicken Shortcake

1 recipe baking powder biscuits
½ cup celery, chopped
4 T. green pepper, chopped
2 T. onion, chopped
2 T. fat
4 T. all-purpose flour
2 cups tomato juice
2 cups cooked chicken, diced
1 tsp. salt
½ tsp. pepper

Preheat oven to 450 degrees.

Make biscuit dough. Roll out one-half of the dough into an eight-inch round. Cut a three-inch circle from center. Roll out remaining dough and fit into an eight-inch cake pan. Brush with melted shortening and place ring on top.

Bake in oven for 15 minutes.

Fry celery, green pepper, and onion in melted fat until tender. Stir in flour. Add tomato juice. Cook slowly. Stir until thick. Add chicken, salt, and pepper.

Serve between shortcake layers.

4 to 6 servings
July 15, 1950

There are undoubledly dozens of chicken pie recipes. In a hurry, you can cook a young broiler or frying chicken and proceed from there. Or you can cook a fowl—it takes more time, but the price is less and the flavor benefits are greater (refer to Chapter Two for more comments about fowl, that "Older Chicken"). In any case, try some of the recipes that follow.

Chicken Pie

½ cup butter
1 cup celery, finely chopped
¾ cup mushrooms, sliced
⅓ cup all-purpose flour
1 tsp. salt
dash pepper
1 cup milk
1½ cups chicken broth
2 cups cooked chicken, coarsely
chopped

Drop Biscuits:

2 cups sifted all-purpose flour
1 T. baking powder
1 tsp. salt
¼ cup shortening
¾ to 1 cup milk

Preheat oven to 425 degrees.

Melt the butter in a large saucepan. Add celery and mushrooms and cook slowly for about five minutes. Stir in the flour, salt, and pepper. Add the milk and chicken broth gradually, stirring constantly. Cook until the sauce is thickened. Stir in the chicken. Pour mixture into a greased two-quart casserole.

Sift the flour, baking powder, and salt together. Cut in shortening, and add the milk to make a drop batter. Drop by spoonsful on top of chicken mixture.

Bake in oven for about 30 minutes.

4 servings
January 3, 1959

Chicken Biscuit

A very palatable dish is chicken biscuit made in the following way: Dress and joint a plump young broiler, salt, pepper, and roll in flour, then put one and one-half cupfuls of boiling water into a small skillet, lay the fowl in and put in a lump of butter half the size of a hen's egg. Cover and set on the stove while you make a little biscuit dough, so that when rolled half an inch thick it will just cover the chicken and fit inside the skillet. Cut across twice with a sharp knife, set in the oven, and by the time the dough bakes the chicken will be done. A young broiler will cook in fifteen minutes; less will do if over a hot fire.

July 11, 1907

Chicken Pie with Vegetables

1 large carrot, cleaned and sliced
6 small potatoes, peeled and quartered
6 small onions, cleaned
1 4- to 5-pound chicken, cooked
2 T. parsley, chopped
¼ cup butter or margarine
2 T. all-purpose flour
1 tsp. salt
⅛ tsp. pepper
2 cups chicken stock
pastry for one-crust pie

Parboil carrots, potatoes, and onions for 15 minutes. Remove chicken from bones and cut in large pieces. Mix chicken, vegetables and parsley in two-quart casserole. Blend butter, flour, salt, and pepper in saucepan. Gradually mix in stock. Cook and stir in pan over medium heat until sauce thickens and boils. Pour over mixture in casserole. Prepare pastry and roll one-eighth-inch thick and one inch larger in diameter than casserole. Cut slits in pastry for escape of steam. Place over chicken mixture. Turn edges under, seal and flute.

Bake in oven at 350 degrees for 40 to 45 minutes, or until crust is browned. Six unbaked biscuits may be used instead of pastry.
6 servings
June 17, 1967

Chicken Turnover

Place a good-sized young chicken in sufficient water to cover and boil until tender enough to slip the bones from the meat; season with salt, pepper and a little celery; bake a light shortcake in a circular pan, split the cake, butter the lower half and arrange the chicken on it; thicken the gravy with a little flour; add a tablespoonful of rich cream and a lump of butter; pour over the chicken on the lower crust and place the top section of the cake over all.
August 2, 1906

Mock Chicken Loaf

Here is a meat loaf that is precooked, and only requires a half to three-quarters of an hour to bake before serving.

Boil one and one-half pounds each of lean pork and veal, in salted water, until the meat becomes tender. When it is cool enough to handle, dice it. Pour three cups of the broth over seven slices of bread, add three well beaten eggs and mix well and mold into the shape of a loaf; then sprinkle crumbs over top and bake.
July 30, 1938

Soubise Chicken

Take a young, fat chicken and prepare for boiling. Cook in a buttered saucepan with a pint of white stock for half an hour, seasoning with salt and pepper to taste. Add a pound of button onions, peeled, and cook half an hour longer, turning the chicken occasionally. At serving time, put the chicken in a deep platter and strain the sauce over it. Make a ring of the boiled onions around the chicken, alternating with small squares of bacon fried to a crisp.
September 17, 1903

Chicken Vegetable Puff

3 T. butter
3 T. all-purpose flour
1 cup milk
1 tsp. salt
¼ tsp. paprika
dash pepper
1 tsp. lemon juice
1 cup cooked chicken, diced
½ package frozen peas, or chopped
    broccoli or asparagus, cooked
4 egg yolks, beaten
4 egg whites, stiffly beaten
1 9-inch unbaked pastry shell

Melt butter and blend in flour. Gradually add milk, stirring constantly over low heat; cook until thick and smooth. Add salt, paprika, pepper, lemon juice, chicken, and peas. Blend egg yolks into creamed mixture. Cool slightly, then fold in egg whites. Pour into pastry shell.

Bake in 325 degree oven for 40 minutes.
4 to 6 servings
March 19, 1966

Luncheon Crepes au Gratin

Crepes:
1½ cups all-purpose flour
½ tsp. salt
3 eggs, beaten
1½ cups milk

Sift flour and salt into bowl. Blend eggs and milk and add to dry ingredients. Beat until smooth. Bake in a lightly-buttered six- or seven-inch skillet, one at a time. As each crepe is baked on both sides, remove from skillet and stack. Keep hot. Fill as follows:

Filling and Sauce:
¼ cup butter
¼ cup all-purpose flour
1 tsp. dry mustard
1 tsp. salt
¼ tsp. pepper
2 cups milk
1 tsp. Worcestershire sauce
1 package frozen, chopped spinach,
*   cooked and well-drained*
1 cup cooked chicken, diced
1 cup sharp American cheese,
*   shredded*

Melt butter in saucepan, blend in flour, mustard, salt, and pepper. Add milk, stirring constantly. Cook until sauce is smooth and thickened. Add Worcestershire sauce. Mix together the cooked spinach and chicken, moisten with about one-half cup sauce. Heat. Place a spoonful of this mixture on each crepe and roll up; place in baking dish. Cover with remaining sauce and top with shredded cheese.

Place under broiler about four inches from heat until cheese is melted. Serve at once.
6 servings
April 4, 1970

Chicken Macaroni Skillet

1 T. salt
3 quarts boiling water
2 cups (8 ounces) elbow macaroni
¼ cup butter
2 cups cooked chicken, diced
1 large onion, sliced
1 medium green pepper, chopped
1 cup mushrooms, sliced
1 clove garlic, crushed
1 cup vegetable juice
¼ cup Parmesan cheese, grated
1½ tsp. basil

Add salt to rapidly boiling water. Gradually add macaroni while water continues to boil. Cook uncovered, stirring occasionally, until tender. Drain in colander. Meanwhile, melt butter; add chicken, onion, green pepper, mushrooms and garlic; mix well. Cook over medium heat, stirring frequently for 10 minutes. Add macaroni; mix well; combine vegetable juice, cheese, and basil and mix well. Pour over macaroni mixture; mix well. Heat to serving temperature, stirring occasionally.
4 to 6 servings
July 20, 1963

Where, as in many families, all go to church and an elaborate dinner is not possible, sometimes a special supper is prepared. For this chicken pie, escalloped potatoes, jam, cake, doughnuts and cheese, or pumpkin or Marlborough pie make a hearty and attractive, little feast which does not overtax the housewife.
The Wisconsin Farmer,
November 21, 1901

Pancakes have been served ever since man discovered that he could make a food by baking crushed grain and water on a hot rock. In the United States we eat flapjacks and griddle cakes, but that's not all. From Mexico we've discovered tortillas; while from Russia, blinis. From the Chinese we have eggrolls and from the French, crepes. All are versions of the pancake, which all too often is confined to breakfast. Try making a delicious and different party dish with filled pancakes as a main dish.

Chicken Filled Main Dish Pancakes

Main Dish Pancakes:
¾ cup all-purpose flour
⅛ tsp. salt
3 eggs, beaten
2 T. butter, melted
¾ cup milk, or as needed
butter, as needed

Sift together flour and salt. Add eggs, a little at a time. Beat until smooth. Add two tablespoons melted butter and mix thoroughly. Add milk, using more or less than three-quarters cup, until the batter is the consistency of heavy cream. Let the batter rest two hours, then beat again.

To make pancakes, melt a teaspoon of butter in a six-inch skillet. Pour in just enough batter to cover the bottom of the pan. As pancake begins to brown around the edges, loosen it by running a spatula around the edge. When pancake appears dry on top, turn with the spatula and brown the other side.

Set aside in a stack, separated by sheets of waxed paper.

Chicken Filling:
2 T. onion, minced
4 T. butter
4 T. all-purpose flour
1 cup milk
1 cup chicken stock

salt and pepper, to taste
1 egg yolk
2 cups cooked chicken, chopped
½ cup cooked mushrooms, chopped
½ cup pimientos, chopped

Saute onion in butter until golden. Blend in flour; stir in three-quarters cup milk and chicken stock; simmer, stirring, until thickened. Beat egg yolk in remaining milk and add. Bring mixture to a simmer and let thicken, but be sure not to boil. Set aside one-half cup of the sauce.

Add chicken, mushrooms, and pimiento to remaining sauce. Spread pancakes with chicken filling and roll; tuck in ends. Place in a shallow baking dish and cover with remaining sauce.

Glaze under a broiler.
12 filled pancakes
March 21, 1959

Festival Tostadas

6 tortillas, cooked until crisp
3 cups refried beans
¾ cup Cheddar cheese, grated
    (about 3 ounces)
lettuce leaves, as needed
3 cups lettuce, shredded
1½ cups cooked chicken, shredded
1½ cups guacamole (recipe follows)
choice of green pepper rings, thinly
    sliced onion rings, radishes, quar-
    tered tomatoes, green olives, or
    ripe olives, as desired for garnish

Place tortillas on an ungreased baking sheet. Spread each with one-half cup refried beans. Top with two tablespoons cheese.

Place under broiler and broil until cheese melts.

Line six plates with lettuce leaves. Place a cooked tortilla on top of lettuce on each plate. Sprinkle each with one-quarter cup each shredded lettuce and chicken. Top with one-quarter cup guacamole. Finish with your choice of garnishes. Serve with purchased taco sauce.
6 servings
February 7, 1976

Don't try to make guacamole too far ahead of time, for avocados discolor and the whole thing will turn an unappetizing brown.

Guacamole

3 ripe avocados, peeled and mashed
1 T. onion, minced
1 T. chili powder
½ tsp. salt
1 tomato, peeled, seeded, and chopped
¼ cup French dressing
lemon juice, as needed

Place avocados in bowl; mix in onions, chili powder, and salt. Add tomato and dressing and mix until smooth. Sprinkle top with lemon juice (to prevent discoloring).

Serve on tostadas.

Guacamole is also good chilled and served as a dip with crisp tortilla chips. February 7, 1976

Popovers are easy and economical to prepare and fun to bring to the table. . . just be sure to serve 'em hot!

Chicken Filled Popovers

Chicken Sauce:
½ cup celery, chopped
1 T. butter
1¼ cups condensed cream of celery
  soup
½ cup water
2 T. pimiento
1 cup cooked chicken, diced

Cook celery in butter until tender, about 10 to 15 minutes. Stir in soup, water, pimiento, and chicken.

When ready to serve, heat to boiling and use to fill popovers.

Popovers:
1 cup sifted all-purpose flour
½ tsp. salt
dash of cayenne pepper
3 eggs, beaten
1 cup milk
1 T. melted shortening
⅓ cup American cheese, shredded

Preheat oven to 375 degrees.

Sift together flour, salt, and cayenne. Combine eggs and milk; add flour mixture and beat to a smooth batter. Add shortening and cheese. Beat three minutes with a rotary beater, or one minute at high speed with an electric mixer. Pour into 12 well-oiled popover pans or custard cups, filling about one-half full.

Bake in oven for one hour, or until firm and brown. Remove from pans, cut slit on side to let out steam. Fill with chicken sauce.

12 filled popovers
October 14, 1967

Chicken Herb Popovers

2 chicken bouillon cubes
½ cup boiling water
½ cup evaporated milk
3 eggs
½ tsp. thyme
1 cup sifted all-purpose flour

Preheat oven to 375 degrees.

Dissolve bouillon cubes in boiling water; cool. Combine with milk, eggs, and thyme in a mixing bowl. Add flour and beat until mixture is smooth.

Fill six well-oiled six-ounce ovenproof custard cups to within ½-inch of tops.

Bake in oven for one hour. Remove from oven; quickly cut slit in side of each popover to let out steam. Return to oven five minutes longer. Remove immediately.

6 large popovers
October 14, 1967

Chicken and Dumplings

A favorite recipe of chicken lovers is chicken and dumplings, which is easy to make with canned chicken.

4 cups canned (or cooked and
chopped) chicken
½ cup cooked onions, chopped
½ cup cooked celery, chopped
½ cup cooked carrots, chopped
½ cup cooked peas
4 cups chicken broth

Combine all ingredients and heat.

Dumplings:

1 egg, slightly beaten
1 T. oil or melted shortening
½ tsp. salt
⅓ cup milk
3 tsp. baking powder
1 cup all-purpose flour

Stir together all ingredients just enough to combine. Drop by spoonfuls on top of hot soup. Cook, covered, for 10 to 15 minutes, depending on the size of the dumplings. Do not peek until the cooking time is completed!
4 servings
October 10, 1970

Volcanos

1 recipe baking powder biscuit dough
1 cup cooked chicken, chopped
2 T. onion, minced
¼ tsp. salt
dash pepper
1 can condensed creamed soup—
mushroom, celery, or chicken
1¼ cups frozen mixed carrots and
peas, slightly thawed

Preheat oven to 450 degrees.
Roll biscuit dough one-quarter inch thick and cut into six-inch squares. Combine chicken, onion, salt, pepper, three-quarters cup of the soup, and vegetable mixture.

Divide filling into six portions and place one on each square of dough. Bring edges of dough together at top. Fold back each corner edge leaving a square opening at top for steam to escape. Crimp the other edges together. This forms a pyramid-like volcano.
Bake in the hot oven for 10 minutes, then reduce heat to 350 degrees and bake 20 minutes longer.
Heat balance of soup and serve as sauce.
6 servings
October 10, 1970

Scalloped Chicken with Stuffing

This is especially good for potluck suppers or feeding large groups. Each pan makes about nine servings.

1 8-ounce package herb stuffing
4 cups cooked chicken, chopped
6 T. butter or margarine
½ cup all-purpose flour
¼ tsp. salt
4 cups chicken broth
6 eggs, slightly beaten

Prepare the stuffing as directed on the package. Spread in a 9 × 13-inch pan. Top with chicken. Melt butter; blend in flour and salt. Add broth and cook until thick. Stir a small amount into eggs, then add eggs to entire mixture. Stir, but do not cook. Pour sauce over chicken. Set in a pan of hot water.
Bake in a 325 degree oven for about one hour, or until knife comes out clean.

Sauce:
1 can cream of mushroom or celery
soup
¼ cup milk
1 cup sour cream
¼ cup pimiento, chopped, if desired

Mix soup, milk, sour cream, and pimiento, if used. Heat to serving temperature.
To serve, cut hot baked scalloped chicken into squares and serve with the sauce.
9 servings
October 10, 1970

Risotto

1 can (4-ounces) mushrooms, sliced
2 chicken bouillon cubes dissolved
   in 2 cups water or 1 10½-ounce
   can condensed chicken consomme
   plus water to make 2 cups
1⅓ cups instant rice
¼ cup butter or margarine
1 cup cooked ground beef or diced
   roast beef
1 cup ham or luncheon meat, diced
   or sliced
1 cup chicken or turkey, diced or sliced
½ cup onion, chopped
¼ cup Parmesan cheese, grated

Drain mushrooms, reserving liquid; measure one-third cup. Place in saucepan with broth. Bring to a boil; stir in rice. Cover, remove from heat, and let stand five minutes. Meanwhile, melt butter in a large skillet. Add beef, ham, chicken, onion, and the mushrooms. Saute until lightly browned. Add rice and cheese; mix gently with a fork.
5 to 6 servings
April 24, 1976

Chicken Noodle Casserole

1 6-ounce package noodles
1 can cream of chicken soup
1 6-ounce can evaporated milk
1 tsp. salt
1½ cups cheddar cheese, shredded
2 cups cooked chicken, diced
1 cup celery, sliced
¼ cup green pepper, chopped
¼ cup pimiento, chopped
1 cup almonds, slivered

Preheat oven to 400 degrees.
   Cook noodles and make nest in casserole. Make sauce of soup, milk, salt, and cheese. Place chicken, celery, green pepper, pimiento, and half of the almonds on nest. Pour sauce over, and top with remaining almonds.
   Bake in oven for 20 minutes.
6 servings
March 23, 1968

Quick Slick Casserole

1 can cream of mushroom soup
1 can cream of chicken soup
½ soup can chicken broth or milk
1 tsp. onion powder
4 cups cooked rice
3 cups cooked chicken, cut into
   large pieces
1 cup cheese, shredded
2 T. pimiento, chopped

Preheat oven to 375 degrees.
   Mix soups and broth. Heat and stir until smooth and hot. Add remaining ingredients. Pour into a buttered two-quart casserole.
   Bake in oven for 25 to 30 minutes.
8 servings
November 25, 1967

Chicken Puff

1 10½-ounce can condensed cream
   of chicken soup
2 cups cooked chicken, finely diced
   or ground
¼ tsp. poultry seasoning
6 egg yolks, well beaten
¼ cup parsley, chopped
6 egg whites, stiffly beaten

Oil a two-quart casserole. Combine soup, chicken, and poultry seasoning; heat. Stir hot mixture slowly into egg yolks. Fold chicken mixture and parsley into egg whites. Pour into casserole. Set in pan of hot water.
   Bake in 350 degree oven for 35 to 45 minutes.
4 to 6 servings
July 8, 1967

33

Chicken Tetrazzini

1 T. salt
3 quarts boiling water
8 ounces spaghetti
¼ cup butter
⅓ cup all-purpose flour
2 cups chicken broth or bouillon
1 cup milk
2 cups cooked chicken, diced
¼ cup pimiento-stuffed green olives,
  sliced
1 4-ounce can sliced mushrooms,
  drained
½ cup Parmesan cheese, grated

Preheat oven to 400 degrees.

Add salt to rapidly boiling water. Gradually add spaghetti so that the water continues to boil. Cook uncovered, stirring occasionally, until tender. Drain. Melt butter over low heat; add flour and blend. Gradually add chicken broth and milk and cook until thickened. Combine half the sauce with spaghetti and turn into a greased one and one-half quart casserole. Add chicken, olives, and mushrooms to remaining sauce. Make a depression in center of spaghetti mixture. Fill with chicken mixture. Sprinkle with cheese.

Bake in oven for about 20 minutes.
4 to 6 servings
March 5, 1960

Casserole Chicken

2 cups cooked chicken, chopped
½ tsp. Worcestershire sauce
1 can cream of chicken soup
1 cup Swiss cheese, shredded
1 small can peas, drained
¼ cup pimiento, diced
½ cup almonds, sliced
hot cooked rice, baking powder biscuits, or toast, as needed

Combine chicken, Worcestershire sauce, soup, cheese, peas, and pimiento. Place in buttered casserole. Top with almonds.

Bake in 350 degree oven for 35 minutes or until bubbly throughout. Serve on top of rice, baking powder biscuits, or toast.
4 servings
May 28, 1966

Chinese Chicken Livers

1 pound chicken livers, rinsed and
  cut in half
2 T. soy sauce
¼ cup (½ stick) butter
¼ cup cornstarch
2 cups chicken broth
1 tsp. salt
¼ cup green onion, chopped
½ cup water chestnuts, sliced
½ cup green pepper, chopped
2 fresh tomatoes, cut into wedges
½ cup toasted almonds

Dip each chicken liver half in soy sauce. Cook livers in butter in a frying pan set over low heat for five minutes, turning often. Remove livers and keep hot. Stir cornstarch into drippings; gradually stir in chicken broth. Cook until thickened, stirring frequently. Add salt, green onion, water chestnuts, green pepper, and tomatoes. Heat until hot. Pour over livers. Garnish with almonds.
4 to 6 servings
February 16, 1974

Express Chicken Almond

1 can (20-ounces) pineapple chunks
6 large chicken breasts
2 T. butter
2 tsp. curry powder
2 tsp. garlic salt
¼ cup water
1 cup sour cream
2 T. green onion, chopped
¼ cup toasted almonds, slivered

Drain pineapple, reserving all syrup. Saute chicken breasts in butter until golden. Stir in curry powder. Sprinkle with garlic salt. Pour pineapple syrup over chicken, add water, cover, and simmer 35 minutes or until tender. Remove chicken to heated serving platter. Stir sour cream into pan juices, but do not boil. Add pineapple chunks and onion. Spoon over chicken. Sprinkle with toasted almonds to serve.
6 servings
April 14, 1973

The special ingredients in this Persian Peach Chicken are low-calorie diet fruits that lend enchantment in flavor without overloading the calorie counts.

Persian Peach Chicken

1 1-pound can low-calorie peach
*   halves*
¼ cup lemon juice
2 T. butter, melted
3 large chicken breasts, cut into halves
salt and pepper, to taste
1 10½-ounce can low-calorie Mandarin
*   oranges or 1 1-pound can low-*
*   calorie cherries*

Press peaches and syrup through a sieve. Mix peaches, lemon juice, and butter. Pat chicken dry; sprinkle with salt and pepper. Put chicken skin side down on a broiler rack.

Broil about six inches away from the source of heat for about 15 minutes. Brush chicken on each side with peach mixture every five minutes for 15 minutes more. Mix remaining peach glaze with oranges (or cherries) and their syrup. Heat to the boiling point and spoon over chicken.
6 servings
February 28, 1976

Chicken and Rice Mandarin

3 broiler-fryer breasts, halved
salt and pepper, to taste
paprika, as desired
3 T. butter or margarine
½ cup onions, chopped
½ cup celery, chopped
3 cups cooked rice
1 can (11 ounces) mandarin orange
*   segments (including juice)*
1 can (5 ounces) water chestnuts,
*   sliced*
½ tsp. poultry seasoning

Season chicken with salt, pepper, and paprika. Saute in butter until brown. Remove from skillet and set aside. In same skillet, cook onions and celery until soft, but not brown. Add rice, orange segments and juice, and poultry seasoning. Adjust seasonings. Turn into buttered baking dish. Arrange chicken on top.

Bake in 375 degree oven for 30 to 40 minutes, or until chicken is tender.
6 servings
January 24, 1976

Drumstick Prune Crown

8 chicken drumsticks
seasoned all-purpose flour, as needed
½ cup butter
2 T. shortening
1 can pineapple slices and juice
½ cup onion, chopped
2 cups cooked rice
1 cup cooked prunes, chopped
1 tsp. poultry seasoning
½ tsp. salt
dash pepper
8 avocado slices

Roll drumsticks in seasoned flour; saute in one-quarter cup of the butter and shortening until golden brown on all sides. Add one-half cup pineapple syrup; cover and simmer 20 to 30 minutes, or until tender. Saute onion in remaining butter until golden brown; add rice, prunes, poultry seasoning, salt, and pepper. Keep hot until chicken is done.

To serve, arrange pineapple slices in circle on plate; place avocado slice on each. Place prune-rice mixture in center of plate; arrange drumsticks on pineapple rings and mound of rice.
8 servings
May 2, 1964

Chicken Fricassee with Biscuits

2 3-pound broilers, cut in serving
    pieces
3 cups water
1 medium onion, chopped
2 stalks celery, finely cut
2 bay leaves
2½ tsp. salt
¼ tsp. pepper
6 carrots, scraped and quartered
12 small white onions
¼ cup all-purpose flour
⅓ cup cold water
12 baked baking powder biscuits, hot

Put chicken in a deep kettle. Add three cups water, onion, celery, bay leaves, salt, and pepper; cover. Bring to a boil. Reduce heat, and simmer 30 minutes, or until chicken is almost tender. Add carrots and onions; bring to boil. Cook, covered, 20 minutes.

Mix flour with cold water. Add some hot broth and stir until smooth. Stir into broth in kettle. Cook, stirring constantly, until thickened. Remove bay leaves. To serve, turn into serving dish; top with biscuits.
6 servings
April 27, 1968

Sesame Seed Chicken Wings

½ cup cornstarch
¼ cup all-purpose flour
¼ cup sugar
1½ tsp. salt
1 tsp. monosodium glutamate
5 T. soy sauce
2 eggs
2 stalks green onion, sliced
2 cloves garlic, minced
2 T. sesame seeds
3 cups corn oil
3 pounds chicken wings

Combine cornstarch, flour, sugar, salt, monosodium glutamate, soy sauce, eggs, onion, garlic, and sesame seeds in a bowl. Then stir in one-half cup corn oil. Discard wing tips, cut at joint, and loosen meat from one joint end. With a sharp knife, push meat over unloosened joint to form ball like a drumstick. Add chicken to mixture and stir to cover all pieces. Marinate two hours.

Heat corn oil to 325 degrees in deep fryer, adding oil to not more than one-third full. Add chicken a few pieces at a time and fry five to seven minutes or until golden brown and fork can be inserted.
4 servings
September 3, 1977

Fresh tomatoes at the height of the summer are a great treat. We are inclined to think of them then in salads only, but fresh tomatoes are delicious cooked as vegetables or combined with other foods. Here is a good example.

Chicken Creole

¼ cup all-purpose flour
1 tsp. salt
pepper, to taste
¼ tsp. paprika
1 4- to 5-pound chicken, cut in serving
    pieces
½ cup fat (chicken fat may be used)
½ cup onion, chopped
½ cup water
¼ cup green pepper, chopped
2½ cups fresh tomatoes
hot cooked rice or noodles, as desired

Combine flour, salt, pepper, and paprika. Roll chicken pieces in the mixture. Brown in melted fat. Add onion; cook for two to three minutes. Add water, cover, and simmer about one hour, or until almost tender. Add more water, if necessary; stir occasionally to keep from sticking. Add green pepper and tomatoes; simmer about 30 minutes longer.

Serve on rice or noodles.
6 to 8 servings
July 18, 1953

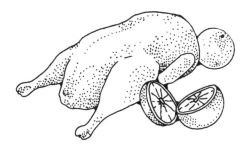

Chicken l'Orange

3 oranges
2 T. orange rind, slivered
¼ tsp. Tabasco®
1 3-pound broiler, cut in serving pieces
salt, to taste
paprika, to taste
4 T. butter or margarine
2 T. all-purpose flour
¼ tsp. salt
⅛ tsp. pepper
1 T. brown sugar
¼ tsp. ginger

Juice two of the oranges. Add rind and Tabasco® to the juice. Add enough water to make one and a half cups; reserve. Sprinkle chicken pieces lightly with salt and paprika; brown in butter in skillet. Remove chicken. Add flour, salt, pepper, brown sugar, and ginger to drippings in skillet; stir to make a smooth paste. Add reserved liquid and cook, stirring constantly, until mixture thickens and comes to a boil. Add chicken pieces. Cover, simmer over low heat until chicken is tender, about 45 minutes. Section remaining orange. Add to chicken last 15 minutes cooking time. Serve with Orange Rice.
4 servings

Orange Rice

3 T. butter
⅔ cup celery, diced with leaves
2 T. onion, chopped
1½ cups water
1 cup orange juice
2 T. orange rind, slivered
1¼ tsp. salt
⅛ tsp. thyme
1 cup uncooked rice

Melt butter in heavy saucepan. Add celery and onion; cook until onion is tender, not brown. Add water, orange juice, rind, salt, and thyme. Bring to a boil; add rice slowly. Cover; reduce heat and cook 25 minutes.
February 16, 1957

Chicken Tahiti

2 pounds chicken, cut in serving pieces
2 T. all-purpose flour
½ tsp. salt
⅛ tsp. pepper
1 small onion, sliced
2 T. butter or margarine
1 can (10¾-ounces) chicken gravy
¼ tsp. allspice
6 canned peach halves
¼ cup maraschino cherries

Dust chicken with flour, salt, and pepper. In skillet, brown chicken and cook onion in butter. Stir in gravy and allspice. Cover, cook over low heat for 45 minutes or until tender. Stir now and then. Add peaches and cherries; heat.
4 servings
September 18, 1971

Fried Italian Chicken

¾ cup enriched corn meal
⅓ cup all-purpose flour
2 tsp. salt
½ tsp. crushed oregano
2 (2½- to 3-pounds) chickens, cut
into serving pieces
½ cup lemon juice

Combine corn meal, flour, salt, and oregano in paper bag. Dip chicken pieces in lemon juice. Shake chicken, a few pieces at a time, in bag until pieces are well coated.

Fry in large skillet in hot shortening, about ½-inch deep, until golden brown on all sides. Reduce heat and cook until tender, 35 to 40 minutes.
6 servings
April 22, 1964

Chicken Thai Style

1 3-pound frying chicken, cut in
serving pieces
¼ cup cooking oil
¼ pound fresh mushrooms, sliced
¼ cup onion, chopped
½ tsp. salt
2 T. preserved ginger, finely chopped
¼ tsp. ground coriander
¼ cup water
4 T. lime juice
2 T. soy sauce
2 T. vinegar
½ tsp. sugar
1½ cup pitted ripe olives
hot cooked rice, as needed

Brown chicken pieces slowly in oil. Remove chicken, then brown mushrooms and onion in drippings. Drain off any excess oil. Return chicken pieces to skillet; sprinkle with salt, ginger, and coriander. Add water, cover and simmer for 10 minutes. Combine lime juice, soy sauce, vinegar, and sugar and sprinkle over chicken. Add drained ripe olives, cover and cook 10 minutes longer, or until tender. Serve with rice.
4 servings
September 18, 1971

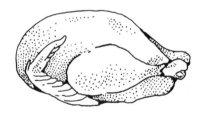

Portuguese Chicken

1 3-pound broiler chicken, cut in
serving pieces
¾ tsp. salt
¼ tsp. pepper
3 T. butter
¼ cup onion, chopped
1 clove garlic, minced
1 T. all-purpose flour
1 8-ounce can tomatoes
¼ cup white wine
1 chicken bouillon cube
2 medium-sized fresh tomatoes
1 cup pitted ripe olives
parsley, as needed for garnish

Season chicken pieces with salt and pepper. Melt butter in skillet and brown chicken. Remove chicken, add onion and garlic to pan and cook until transparent. Stir in the flour. Add canned tomatoes, wine, and bouillon cube. Cook, stirring constantly, until sauce boils and is thickened. Return chicken to pan, cover tightly and cook over low heat about 30 minutes.

Core and cut fresh tomatoes into eighths. Add to pan along with ripe olives. Cover and cook five minutes longer. Garnish with parsley.

4 servings
September 18, 1971

Filipino Chicken

½ cup butter
1 2- to 3-pound fryer, cut into serving
pieces
¾ tsp. salt
pepper, to taste
1 cup ham, cubed
1 large onion, sliced
1 clove garlic, crushed
1 cup uncooked rice
3½ cups cooked tomatoes
2½ cups cooked lima beans, undrained
¼ cup pimiento, chopped
3 hard-cooked eggs, quartered

Melt butter in a heavy skillet. Season chicken with salt and pepper. Brown on both sides. Remove from skillet. Add ham, onion, and garlic; cook for three minutes. Add rice, tomatoes, lima beans, and pimiento, pressing the rice under the liquid. Replace chicken on top of the mixture. Cover and cook over low heat for 30 to 40 minutes, or until chicken is fork tender.

To serve, garnish with eggs.

4 to 6 servings
May 3, 1958

When flouring chicken for frying, spread a paper on your work table, sift the flour over this, lay on your chicken and sprinkle again. It is now ready for the hot fat, which I always salt and pepper before putting in the meat. Gather up your paper and consign to the flames. You do not have a pasty place to wash, or any waste flour.
The Prairie Farmer,
November 15, 1914

Saucy Cranberry Chicken

1 2½-pound fryer, cut into serving
   pieces
½ cup sifted all-purpose flour
2 tsp. paprika
2¼ tsp. salt
1⅜ tsp. ground cinnamon
⅛ tsp. ground nutmeg
¾ tsp. ground ginger
¼ tsp. onion salt
⅛ tsp. ground thyme
⅛ tsp. pepper
⅓ cup butter
1 T. orange juice
1½ cups jellied cranberry sauce
½ cup water
4 whole cloves
½ cup almonds, slivered (optional)

Dry chicken pieces thoroughly. Sift
together twice flour, paprika, salt, cinnamon, nutmeg, ginger, onion salt, thyme, and
pepper. Heat butter in an 11-inch skillet.
Roll pieces of chicken in flour mixture. Place
skin side down, big pieces in the center, in
skillet. Brown slowly 15 to 20 minutes. Turn
occasionally to prevent sticking. Add
orange juice. Cover and cook slowly for 20
minutes, turning occasionally. Pour off
excess fat.

In a small saucepan, blend cranberry
sauce, water, and cloves together. Heat, stirring constantly, until sauce is melted and
mixture is blended. Pour one-half of this
mixture over the chicken. Cover and cook
slowly 15 to 20 minutes, or until chicken is
fork-tender. Turn when necessary to prevent sticking. Add the rest of the cranberry
mixture and simmer, uncovered, until a
thick sauce is formed. Add almonds, if used.
4 to 5 servings
October 24, 1970

Raisin Rice Chicken Skillet

8 frying chicken pieces
3 T. shortening
1 medium onion, chopped
1 cup rice
⅔ cup dark seedless raisins
½ tsp. oregano
1 tsp. garlic salt
½ tsp. paprika
¼ tsp. pepper
2 cups canned tomatoes
2 chicken bouillon cubes
1½ cups boiling water

Brown chicken pieces slowly in shortening
in heavy skillet. Push pieces to side of
skillet; add onion and cook a few minutes
to soften. Add rice, raisins, seasonings, and
tomatoes. Dissolve bouillon cubes in water;
add to mixture. Stir to mix well, distribut-
ing chicken throughout rice. Cover tightly;
simmer until chicken is tender and rice has
absorbed all liquid, about 45 minutes.
4 generous servings
November 9, 1968

40

Almost everyone has a favorite way of frying chicken. Two examples follow.

Chicken Fried in Batter

1 frying chicken, cut into serving pieces
1 cup all-purpose flour
¼ tsp. salt
2 tsp. baking powder
1 egg, beaten
1 cup cream or evaporated milk
salt, to taste
frying fat, as needed

Dry chicken pieces. Sift together flour, salt, and baking powder. Add egg and cream and mix together. Sprinkle chicken lightly with salt and dip into batter.

Fry in deep fat at 325 degrees until a golden brown.
4 to 6 servings
July 1, 1950

Southern Fried Chicken

A native of South Carolina insists chicken is not fit to eat unless it is fried southern style. Here is her method, and no one will consider time or chicken wasted when it is brought to the table golden, tender, and delicious.

1 frying chicken, cut into serving pieces
¾ cup all-purpose flour
2 tsp. salt
1 tsp. paprika
½ tsp. pepper
frying fat, as needed to make 1-inch
*   of fat in frying pan*
1 cup hot water
all-purpose flour, as needed
1 cup cream
1 cup milk
½ cup water
salt and pepper, to taste

Dry chicken pieces. Put flour, salt, paprika, and pepper into a paper sack. Place chicken inside and shake until thoroughly covered with flour.

Heat frying fat in heavy frying pan, and brown chicken on all sides. Fry until chicken is barely tender. Add one cup hot water, cover pan, and cook until chicken is done.

Remove chicken from pan. Measure fat; to each four tablespoons fat add two tablespoons flour and blend until smooth. Add cream, milk, and one-half cup water. Add salt and pepper. Cook to consistency of gravy.

To serve, pour gravy over chicken.
4 to 6 servings
July 1, 1950

Spicy Chicken in Barbecue Sauce

salt, pepper, and all-purpose flour,
*   as needed for coating chicken*
2- to 2½-pounds chicken, cut in
*   serving pieces*
⅓ cup fat or salad oil
2 T. brown sugar
1 T. paprika
1 tsp. salt
1 tsp. dry mustard
¼ tsp. chili powder
few grains cayenne pepper
2 T. Worcestershire sauce
1 cup tomato juice
¼ cup chili sauce or catsup
¼ cup vinegar
½ cup onion, chopped

Combine salt, pepper, and flour. Roll chicken pieces in mixture until thoroughly coated. Heat fat in ovenproof pan and brown chicken on all sides over moderate heat, about 20 minutes.

Meanwhile, combine brown sugar, paprika, salt, mustard, chili powder, cayenne, Worcestershire, tomato juice, chili sauce, vinegar, and onion; cook over low heat for 15 minutes. Pour sauce over browned chicken; cover pan.

Bake in 325 degree oven about 45 minutes, or until tender. Uncover pan and place under broiler. Broil 15 minutes or until meat is brown.
6 servings
July 2, 1960

Tangy Chicken

2 cups pancake mix
½ tsp. dry mustard
1 tsp. salt
1 8-ounce can tomato sauce
⅔ cup water
4 tsp. Worcestershire sauce
⅔ cup dill pickle, chopped
2 2½-pound frying chickens, cut up

Heat oil in a deep fat fryer to 375 degrees.

For batter dip, combine pancake mix, mustard, and salt in a bowl. Add tomato sauce, water, Worcestershire, and pickle; beat with a rotary beater about two minutes. Dip chicken in batter; drain.

Fry in hot deep fat for two to three minutes, or until golden brown. Drain on absorbent paper. Place browned chicken in a shallow baking pan.

Bake in 350 degree oven about 40 minutes, or until tender.
6 servings
June 17, 1967

Polynesian Fried Chicken

1 egg
½ cup milk
2 tsp. salt
1 frying chicken, cut into serving pieces
½ cup orange juice
3½-ounce can coconut flakes
½ cup butter
1 orange, peeled and sectioned

Preheat oven to 400 degrees.

Combine egg, milk, and salt. Dip chicken into mixture. Dip into orange juice, then into coconut to coat thoroughly.

In oven, melt butter in a shallow baking pan. Remove pan from oven and place in it the pieces of chicken. Coat with butter, then bake skin side down in a single layer. Bake for 30 minutes, then turn chicken. Bake another 30 minutes, or until tender.

To serve, garnish hot chicken with orange sections.
4 to 6 servings
May 3, 1958

Lemon Leilani Baked Chicken

1 2½-pound chicken, cut in serving
pieces
salt and pepper, to taste
2 to 3 T. salad oil
1 medium onion, chopped
½ cup celery, chopped
1 8-ounce can crushed pineapple,
well drained
1 tsp. grated lemon peel
⅓ cup catsup
2 T. brown sugar
1 tsp. prepared mustard
2 tsp. soy sauce
½ tsp. salt

Season chicken with salt and pepper. In skillet, brown chicken in oil; transfer to a 13×9×2-inch baking dish. In the same skillet, saute onion and celery until tender, using additional oil if necessary. Add remaining ingredients; bring to a boil. Pour over chicken.

Bake, uncovered, in 350 degree oven for 50 minutes, or until tender.
4 servings
March 27, 1976

Indian Chicken

2 chickens, halved
2 cups onion, chopped
2 green peppers, chopped
2 tomatoes, peeled and chopped
2 tsp. salt
freshly ground pepper, to taste
pinch garlic powder
1 tsp. tumeric
½ tsp. cinnamon
1 T. coriander
curry powder, to taste
⅓ cup butter, melted
2 cups chicken stock

Preheat oven to 375 degrees.

Place chickens skin side up in a shallow baking pan. Sprinkle with onions, green peppers, tomatoes, salt, pepper, garlic powder, tumeric, cinnamon, coriander, and curry powder. Pour melted butter over all. Add stock.

Bake in oven, basting frequently, for 50 minutes. Serve with Pineapple Curried Rice (or substitute plain white rice).

4 to 6 servings

Pineapple Curried Rice

1 cup long grain white rice
1 cup water
1 cup pineapple juice
1 tsp. curry powder
1 tsp. salt
2 T. butter or margarine

Combine rice, water, juice, curry powder, and salt in a saucepan. Heat to boiling, add butter, cover pan, and cook 18 minutes on medium low heat without removing cover.

Fluff with fork and serve.*

4 servings

*This recipe is excellent served cold, mixed with mayonnaise, as a base for a salad. You can also substitute orange juice for a different taste.

February 19, 1975

Oven Fried Chicken and Bananas

1 cup all-purpose flour
2 tsp. salt
¼ tsp. pepper
1 tsp. thyme
1 frying chicken, cut in serving
    pieces
½ cup butter
2 slightly green-tipped bananas
juice of 1 lemon
graham cracker crumbs, as needed

Preheat oven to 400 degrees.

Combine flour, salt, pepper, and thyme. Dip chicken pieces into mixture. Melt butter in a shallow baking pan. As pieces of floured chicken are placed in the pan, coat with butter, and turn skin down.

Bake in oven for 40 minutes. Remove pan from oven. Turn chicken and move pieces toward one end, clearing one-fourth of the pan. Peel bananas and cut in half crosswise. Sprinkle with lemon juice and roll in graham cracker crumbs. Place in pan with the chicken.

Return to hot oven and bake for approximately 20 minutes, or until chicken is fork tender.

4 to 6 servings
May 3, 1958

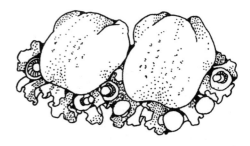

43

Chicken in Egg Puff

4 T. fat
1 2½-pound broiler, cut into serving
    pieces
1 cup all-purpose flour
1 tsp. baking powder
¾ tsp. salt
3 eggs, well-beaten
1 cup milk
2 T. fat, melted

Preheat oven to 375 degrees.

Melt four tablespoons fat; add chicken and cook until light brown. Sift together flour, baking powder, and salt. Blend together eggs and milk and pour into a well made in the flour mixture. Add two tablespoons melted fat. Blend slowly, then thoroughly. Pour into baking dish. Arrange chicken on batter.

Bake in oven for 45 minutes.

4 to 6 servings
September 16, 1961

Chicken Pacific

2 cups sour cream
1 tsp. thyme
½ tsp. garlic powder
1 tsp. paprika
2 tsp. salt
1 2-pound chicken, cut into serving
    pieces
1½ cups cornflake crumbs
¼ cup (½ stick) butter
1 cup canned shrimp–tiny size
¼ cup ripe olives, diced

Combine one cup sour cream, thyme, garlic powder, paprika, and salt. Dip chicken into the sour cream mixture, then into cornflake crumbs. Place chicken, skin side down, in a baking dish.

Bake in a 350 degree oven for 45 minutes.

While the chicken is baking, add shrimp to remaining sour cream and add olives. Pour this sauce over the chicken during the last 10 minutes of baking time.

Serve hot.

4 servings
April 3, 1965

Chicken Paprikash

¼ cup butter
1 frying chicken (3½ pounds), cut
    into serving pieces
½ cup onion, chopped
¼ cup all-purpose flour
2 T. paprika
2 tsp. salt
¼ tsp. pepper
1 can (13½ ounces) chicken broth
2 cups sour cream
1 T. Worcestershire sauce
1 package (8 ounces) medium noodles,
    cooked and drained

Melt butter in large frypan. Saute chicken pieces until lightly brown. Remove chicken pieces from pan; add onion to pan drippings. Blend in flour, paprika, salt, and pepper. Add chicken broth and cook, stirring constantly, until thick and smooth. Stir in sour cream and Worcestershire sauce. Mix one-half of sauce with noodles and pour into shallow three-quart casserole. Arrange chicken on noodles. Spoon remaining sauce over chicken pieces.

Bake in 325 degree oven about one hour, or until chicken is tender and noodles hot and bubbly.

6 servings
July 18, 1975

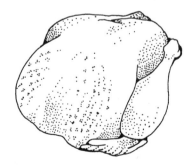

Orange Baked Chicken

1 2½- to 3- pound frying chicken,
*   cut into serving pieces*
salt and pepper, to taste
¼ cup all-purpose flour
¼ cup shortening or salad oil
1 cup fresh orange juice
½ cup chili sauce
¼ cup green pepper, chopped
1 tsp. prepared mustard
½ to 1 tsp. garlic salt
2 T. soy sauce
1 T. molasses
3 medium oranges, peeled, sliced
*   into half-cartwheels (cut peeled*
*   oranges crosswise, then in half)*

Season chicken pieces with salt and pepper
and coat lightly with flour. Heat shortening in large skillet, add chicken pieces and
brown lightly on all sides. Remove browned
chicken to three-quart casserole; drain fat
from pan. To skillet, add remaining ingredients except orange slices and simmer
gently for two to three minutes. Pour sauce
over chicken.

Cover and bake in 350 degree oven for
50 to 60 minutes. Just before serving, add
oranges.
4 servings
February 3, 1968

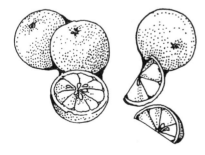

A perfect accompaniment to Orange Baked
Chicken.

Orange Glazed Fresh Carrots

3 T. fresh orange juice
1½ T. sugar
¼ cup butter or margarine
6 whole cloves
¼ tsp. salt
4½ cups carrots, sliced and cooked
*   only until crisp-tender (about 11*
*   carrots)*
fresh parsley, chopped, as needed

Combine orange juice, sugar, butter, cloves,
and salt in a saucepan. Cook until butter
is melted and sauce is hot. Remove cloves
and pour mixture over hot carrots. Garnish
with fresh parsley.
5 servings
February 3, 1968

Peachy Oven-Fried Chicken

1 2½- to 3-pound broiler-fryer chicken,
*   cut into serving pieces*
⅔ cup all-purpose flour
1½ tsp. ground ginger
1 tsp. salt
2 T. butter
2 T. salad oil
1 can (29 ounces) cling peach
*   halves, drained*

Rinse chicken; pat dry. Combine flour,
ginger, and salt. Dredge chicken in flour
mixture. Melt butter and oil in shallow baking pan. Arrange chicken, skin side down,
in pan. Do not stack pieces.

Bake in 350 degree oven for 45 minutes.
Turn; place one peach half on each piece.
Return to oven and bake 15 minutes longer.
4 to 6 servings
November 13, 1976

Oven Crisp Chicken

¾ cup cracker meal
½ cup Parmesan cheese, grated
½ cup ground pecans or walnuts
¾ tsp. salt
2 eggs
1 cup buttermilk
1 broiler-fryer chicken (2½- to
    3-pounds), cut into serving pieces
melted butter, as needed

Preheat oven to 400 degrees.
   Combine cracker meal, cheese, nuts, and salt. Beat together eggs and buttermilk. Roll chicken in cracker meal mixture until it picks up a fine even coat. Dip into egg mixture; then roll again in cracker meal to coat thoroughly. Place in a single layer in a 13×9×2-inch baking pan; brush lightly with melted butter.
   Bake, brushing occasionally with melted butter, one hour, or until chicken is tender and well browned. If coated chicken is stored in refrigerator before baking, allow one and a quarter hours for baking.
4 servings
July 27, 1974

Maple-Cream Chicken

1 egg, beaten
¼ cup milk
1 2-pound chicken, cut into serving
    pieces
¾ cup corn flake crumbs
5 T. cooking oil
1 cup light cream
1 cup milk
½ cup maple syrup
pineapple slices, as needed
currant jelly, as needed

Preheat oven to 375 degrees.
   Combine egg and milk. Put chicken pieces into this mixture and roll in crumbs. Brown chicken in hot oil and place pieces in shallow baking pan. Combine cream, 1 cup milk, and maple syrup and pour over the chicken.

Put chicken into oven, turning pieces after ½ hour, and bake until tender, about 1½ hours.
   To serve, garnish with pineapple slices and currant jelly surrounding the chicken on a platter.
4 servings
April 9, 1963

Crispy Oven Fried Lemon Chicken

1 broiler-fryer, 2½- to 3-pounds, cut
    into serving pieces
½ tsp. salt
½ tsp. onion salt
½ tsp. thyme, crushed
½ tsp. marjoram, crushed
2 tsp. grated lemon peel
⅓ cup fresh lemon juice
½ cup water
lemon quarters
paprika, as needed
parsley, finely snipped, as needed

Preheat oven to 400 degrees.
   Sprinkle chicken pieces with salt, rubbing well. Place chicken in shallow baking dish, skin side down. Combine onion salt, thyme, marjoram, lemon peel, juice, and water; pour over chicken.
   Bake in oven, uncovered, about 40 minutes. Turn chicken and continue baking, basting with pan drippings once or twice, until chicken is done and skin is crispy, about 35 minutes longer.
   Dust one cut side of lemon quarters with paprika, the other side with parsley bits. Garnish serving platter with the lemon pieces.
4 servings
September 7, 1968

Oven Fried
Chicken a la Creole

¼ cup butter
⅓ cup all-purpose flour
3 tsp. salt
1 tsp. paprika
¼ tsp. poultry seasoning
¼ tsp. black pepper
1 fryer chicken, 2½- to 3½-pounds,
    cut into serving pieces
1 cup uncooked rice
½ cup green pepper, chopped
½ cup onion, chopped
3 cups hot chicken broth, made by
    cooking backs and necks in water
2 large tomatoes, cut into wedges

Preheat oven to 400 degrees.

Place butter in large, all-metal skillet or baking pan, about 12×9×2 inches; put in oven until butter melts. Meanwhile, coat pieces of chicken with mixture of flour, one and one-half teaspoon salt, paprika, poultry seasoning, and one-eighth teaspoon pepper. Place chicken in hot melted butter, skin side down.

Bake, uncovered, 25 minutes.

Arrange rice, green pepper, and onion under chicken, turning the chicken skin side up. Sprinkle rice with remaining salt and pepper. Pour hot chicken broth over rice, making sure all rice is under broth. Arrange tomato wedges over chicken and rice. Return to oven and bake, uncovered, 45 minutes longer, or until rice is tender. If mixture becomes too dry, add small amount of chicken broth or water.

6 servings
August 18, 1956

Baked Chicken with
Peach Sauce

1 cup cereal crumbs
1 tsp. salt
½ tsp. paprika
1 (3- to 3½-pound) frying chicken,
    cut into serving pieces
⅓ cup butter, melted
1 can sliced peaches
1½ T. vinegar
2 tsp. sugar
1½ tsp. cornstarch
½ tsp. cinnamon
¼ tsp. salt
⅛ tsp. nutmeg

Combine cereal crumbs, salt, and paprika. Dip chicken in butter, then in cereal mixture. Place pieces in shallow two-quart baking dish, skin side up. Pour remaining butter over chicken. Cover with foil; crimp edges onto edge of dish.

Bake in 325 degree oven for 25 minutes. Remove foil; bake until chicken is browned and tender, 35 to 40 minutes longer. Combine remaining ingredients to make sauce. Cook, stirring constantly, until thickened and clear. Pour over chicken during last 10 minutes of cooking time.

4 servings
July 13, 1968

Lime-Broiled Chicken

½ cup lime juice
½ cup corn oil
1 tsp. monosodium glutamate
1 tsp. seasoned salt
1 tsp. garlic salt
1 tsp. crushed tarragon
¼ tsp. pepper
1 T. onion, grated
1 broiler-fryer chicken, cut in serving
  pieces

Mix lime juice, oil, monosodium glutamate, seasoned salt, garlic salt, tarragon, pepper, and onion. Brush chicken generously with marinade. Place chicken, skin side down, on rack on pan in lowest part of broiler.

Broil, turning every 10 minutes and basting with marinade, about 40 minutes, or until brown and fork can be inserted with ease.

4 servings
September 3, 1977

Italian Chicken-Romano Style

¼ cup shortening
1 broiler-fryer chicken, cut in serving
  pieces
1 small onion, chopped
1 clove garlic, minced
½ cup green pepper, chopped
1 1-pound can tomato puree
½ tsp. salt
½ tsp. oregano
¼ tsp. basil
⅛ tsp. pepper
¼ cup Romano cheese, grated

Heat shortening in skillet. Pat chicken dry with paper towel. Brown chicken in hot fat. Remove chicken and add onion, garlic, and green pepper to fat; saute. Add tomato puree, salt, oregano, basil, and pepper. Mix well. Return chicken to skillet and spoon sauce over it. Top with grated cheese.

Bake, uncovered, in 350 degree oven for 50 to 60 minutes, or until tender.

4 servings
September 18, 1971

Moa Hawaiian

1 3-pound frying chicken, cut in
  serving pieces
1 tsp. salt
1 egg
⅓ cup frozen pineapple-orange juice
  concentrate, thawed
1 cup cornflake crumbs
½ cup coconut, shredded
½ tsp. curry powder
¼ cup butter or margarine, melted

Arrange chicken pieces in shallow baking pan; sprinkle with salt. Beat egg with pineapple-orange concentrate in small bowl and pour over chicken pieces. Let stand in refrigerator about an hour, turning chicken once. In shallow dish or pie pan mix cornflake crumbs with coconut and curry powder. Drain chicken pieces slightly; coat with crumb mixture. Place skin side up in single layer in foil-lined shallow pan. Drizzle with melted butter.

Bake in 350 degree oven about one hour or until tender. Serve on heated plates.

6 to 8 servings
September 18, 1971

Oriental Honeyed Chicken

1 broiler-fryer chicken, cut in serving
  pieces
1 egg, beaten
2 T. butter, melted
2 T. soy sauce
2 T. lemon juice
¼ cup honey
salt and pepper, to taste

Arrange chicken pieces in shallow baking pan. In a bowl combine egg, butter, soy sauce, lemon juice, honey, salt, and pepper. Mix well. Pour sauce over chicken, turning pieces to coat them.

Bake, uncovered, in 300 degree oven for one hour or until tender. Turn and baste occasionally. Serve hot or cold.

6 servings
September 18, 1971

Sweet 'n' Smoky Oven Barbecued Chicken

1 broiler-fryer, quartered
1 large onion, sliced
1 tsp. hickory smoked salt
¼ tsp. pepper

Barbecue Sauce:
½ cup catsup
½ cup corn oil
½ cup maple syrup
¼ cup vinegar
2 T. prepared mustard

Preheat oven to 375 degrees.

Place chicken, skin side up, in shallow baking pan. Tuck onion slices in and around the chicken. Sprinkle with smoked salt and pepper.

Bake uncovered in oven for 30 minutes. Meanwhile, make barbecue sauce by mixing together ingredients listed. Pour barbecue sauce over chicken and bake 30 minutes longer or until done.
4 servings
March 20, 1976

Country Chicken

4 chicken breasts
2 packages frozen broccoli spears
2 cans cheddar cheese soup
½ cup blue cheese, crumbled (about 3 ounces)
¼ cup parmesan cheese
3 green pepper rings

Gently simmer chicken until done. Remove meat from bones. Cut or tear meat into large pieces.

Cut broccoli length-wise into thin stalks. In a buttered casserole place a layer of chicken, then a layer of broccoli. Spoon soup over broccoli, sprinkle blue cheese over top. Alternate layers until chicken, broccoli, and blue cheese are used. Spoon last cheese soup over top; sprinkle with parmesan cheese.

Bake in 350 degree oven for about 45 minutes or until mixture is lightly browned and bubbly. Garnish with pepper rings.

Turkey may be substituted for the chicken, or asparagus for the broccoli, if desired.
4 servings
February 5, 1972

Chicken Kiev

Egg Batter:
1 cup milk
1 egg
1 T. all-purpose flour
½ tsp. salt

6 whole breasts of chicken, boned
butter, as needed
all-purpose flour, salt, and pepper, as needed
½ cup mushrooms, sliced
1½ cups sour cream
½ cup chives, chopped

Prepare batter by combining the milk, egg, flour, and salt. Set aside.

Wash chicken and dry thoroughly. Split the long way of the breast and insert a pat of butter in each slit. Roll up tight and fasten with skewer or toothpick. Roll in seasoned flour and dip in batter. Roll lightly in seasoned flour again and fry in butter until brown and tender. Drain off the fat left in the pan and add the mushrooms. Simmer one minute, add the sour cream and chives. Simmer until it starts to boil; place in a chafing dish and place the cooked breasts on top. Serve at once.
6 servings
May 21, 1966

Chicken Ratatouille

1 cup corn oil
2 whole chicken breasts, boned and
*   cut into 1-inch pieces*
2 small zucchini, unpared and sliced
1 small eggplant, peeled and cut in
*   1-inch cubes*
1 green pepper, cut in 1-inch pieces
1 large onion, sliced
½ pound mushrooms, sliced
1 (16 ounce) can tomatoes
2 tsp. monosodium glutamate
1 tsp. dried basil
1 tsp. dried parsley
½ tsp. pepper
hot cooked rice, as needed

Heat corn oil in large fry pan. Add chicken to pan and saute about two minutes on each side. Add zucchini, eggplant, green pepper, onion, and mushrooms. Cook, stirring occasionally, about 15 minutes or until tender crisp. Add tomatoes and stir carefully. Add monosodium glutamate, basil, parsley, and pepper, and simmer about five minutes or until fork can be inserted in chicken with ease.

Serve on large platter with rice.
4 servings
September 3, 1977

Chinese Chicken and Potatoes

2 T. salad oil
2 medium potatoes, peeled and thinly
*   sliced*
4 chicken breast halves, boned,
*   skinned, and cut into strips*
1 package (6 ounces) frozen snow peas
1 can (16 ounces) bean sprouts,
*   drained*
3 stalks celery, thinly sliced
4 large mushrooms, sliced
½ cup chicken broth
3 T. soy sauce
1 T. cornstarch

In large skillet or wok, over medium-high heat, in hot oil, cook potatoes and chicken, stirring frequently, about five minutes. Add vegetables; cook, stirring, until tender-crisp. In bowl, combine broth and soy sauce. Blend in cornstarch. Pour into skillet and cook, stirring, until sauce is smooth and thickened.
4 servings
March 26, 1977

Curried Chicken Cantonese

3 T. vegetable oil
½ tsp. salt
1 3- to 4-pound fryer chicken, skinned,
*   boned, and cut into 2-inch slices*
½ cup onions, sliced
1 clove garlic, crushed
2 stalks celery, diced
1 tsp. monosodium glutamate
½ cup green pepper, cut into 1-inch
*   squares*
3 tsp. curry powder
2 cups chicken stock or broth
2 tsp. soy sauce
2 T. cornstarch (optional)
2 T. cold water (optional)

Pour oil and salt in wok or skillet, or in electric skillet which has been preheated to 375 degrees. Add one-half of chicken and stir-fry for three or four minutes or until browned. Push up the side. Repeat with remaining chicken. Add onions, garlic, celery, monosodium glutamate, green pepper, curry powder, chicken stock, and soy sauce. Stir all ingredients together. When mixture reaches a boil, reduce heat and simmer covered for 30 minutes, or until chicken is tender.

If thicker sauce is desired, add cornstarch mixed to a paste with cold water. Add gradually. Stir and mix until gravy thickens.

Serve with (or over) hot steamed rice.
4 to 5 servings
July 12, 1975

Chicken Breasts with Swiss Cheese

3 large chicken breasts, halved and
    boned
2 packages Swiss cheese slices–
    enough for 9 slices
6 slices boiled or baked ham
1 egg, slightly beaten
2 T. cold water
all-purpose flour, as needed
3 T. butter
1 tsp. green onion, chopped
⅓ cup water
5 large tomatoes, cut into thin wedges
1 cup light cream
2 small cans mushrooms
½ cup milk, or as needed
2 T. butter
2 T. all-purpose flour
½ tsp. salt
¼ tsp. pepper
fresh parsley, finely chopped, as needed
hot cooked rice or toast points, as
    desired

Skin the chicken; separate the top fillet from the one beneath. Flatten each with a rolling pin. Cut cheese slices in half, crosswise. Make a roll of three half slices. Overlap one small and one large fillet. Place cheese roll over small fillet and roll it around the cheese; fasten ends with a toothpick.

Combine egg and cold water. Dip chicken in egg mixture; roll in flour. Melt three tablespoons butter in a frying pan; fry chicken rolls. Remove from pan and place each roll on a ham slice. Add onion and one-third cup water to pan drippings. Cook until the liquid is reduced by one-half. Add tomatoes and boil briskly until most of the liquid is boiled away. Remove from heat. Stir in cream. Return to low heat and cook until the liquid is again reduced by half. Drain mushrooms, reserving liquid. Add enough milk to make one cup.

Melt 2 tablespoons butter. Blend in flour, salt, and pepper. Remove from heat and gradually add mushroom-milk mixture, stirring constantly. Return to low heat, stirring, and cook until thickened. Pour into frying pan and blend well. Add mushrooms and heat. Pour over chicken rolls and sprinkle with parsley.

Serve hot with rice or over toast points.
6 servings
September 16, 1961

Chicken and Walnuts

½ cup walnuts
hot fat for frying, as needed
2 T. cornstarch
½ tsp. ground ginger
¼ tsp. powdered garlic
1 tsp. sugar
½ tsp. salt
2 T. butter
1 pound chicken breasts, boned
5 T. soy sauce
¾ cup water
½ cup apple juice
1 4-ounce can diced bamboo shoots

Prepare walnuts by boiling in water for five minutes. Remove skin and dry meats. Fry in hot oil until golden brown. Set aside.

Combine cornstarch, ginger, garlic, sugar, and salt; roll chicken in mixture. Save any portion of mixture that is left over. Melt butter in saucepan, and brown chicken. Combine two tablespoons of the soy sauce, one-half cup of the water, and one-quarter cup of the apple juice. Pour this mixture over the browned chicken. Cover, and simmer 20 to 30 minutes. Stir once or twice while cooking.

Add bamboo shoots to chicken mixture. Combine one-quarter cup water, one-quarter cup apple juice, and three tablespoons soy sauce with any remaining dry mixture. Add liquid mixture to chicken; stir until thick.

Serve hot, garnished with fried walnuts.
4 servings
May 3, 1958

Chicken and Asparagus

6 T. oil
3 whole chicken breasts, skinned,
  boned, and sliced into thin strips
  about 1½-inches long
½-pound asparagus, split lengthwise
  and sliced into ½-inch lengths
1 bunch green onions, trimmed and
  sliced thin (¾ cup)
3 T. pimiento, chopped
2 T. ripe olives, chopped
1 can (3 or 4 ounces) sliced
  mushrooms
1 can condensed chicken broth
1 tsp. ground ginger
½ tsp. salt
1 tsp. sugar
2 T. cornstarch
⅓ cup dry sherry
3 T. soy sauce
4 cups cooked rice

Heat four tablespoons oil in large skillet. Stir
in chicken. Saute, stirring several times, for
four minutes or until chicken turns white.
Remove from skillet to bowl. Keep warm.

Heat remaining oil in same skillet. Stir
in asparagus, green onions, pimiento, and
olives. Saute two minutes. Stir in chicken,
mushrooms and liquid, chicken broth,
ginger, salt, and sugar. Cover. Simmer
three minutes. Mix cornstarch, sherry, and
soy sauce in a cup until smooth. Stir into
mixture in skillet. Cook, stirring until mixture thickens, for one minute.

Serve over hot rice.
6 servings
April 22, 1960

Celestial Gold Chicken

Filling:
2 cups cabbage, finely shredded
¼ cup green onion, finely chopped
¼ cup butter
1 cup bean sprouts, rinsed, chopped,
  and drained
1 cup water chestnuts, finely chopped
1½ T. pimiento, chopped
½ tsp. salt
2 tsp. sugar
¼ tsp. dried basil leaves
dash allspice

4 large chicken breasts, split,
  skinned, and boned
salt and pepper, to taste
all-purpose flour, as needed
2 eggs, slightly beaten
1 T. water
fine dry bread crumbs, as needed
⅓ cup butter

Sauce:
¼ cup onion, chopped
1 clove garlic, minced
2 T. butter
¾ cup chicken broth
1 cup whipping cream
2 tsp. soy sauce
3 T. flour
Chow mein noodles, as needed

Prepare Filling: Cook cabbage and green onions in butter until tender, about five minutes. Add bean sprouts, water chestnuts, pimiento, salt, sugar, basil, and allspice; heat until hot. Cool.

Cover each chicken breast with plastic wrap; flatten with flat side of meat pounder or rolling pin to one-eighth-inch thickness, taking care not to tear chicken. Peel off plastic wrap. Sprinkle chicken with salt and pepper. Place one-quarter cup of the filling in center of each piece of chicken. Roll up tightly, folding in the ends. Dip chicken in flour, shaking off excess. Next dip in eggs and water which have been blended together; then in bread crumbs, coating well. Brown in butter in skillet. Arrange in oiled baking pan.

Prepare Sauce: Cook onion and garlic in butter until onion is golden, about three minutes. Blend in one-half cup broth, cream, and soy sauce. Pour sauce over chicken.

Cover and bake in 350 degree oven for 45 minutes. Remove cover and bake 15 minutes more or until tender. Remove chicken to serving dish; keep warm. Combine remaining chicken broth and flour; mix until smooth. Blend into pan juices. Cook over medium heat, stirring constantly, until thickened. Pour over chicken. Garnish with chow mein noodles.

8 servings
January 12, 1974

A "must" in Chinese cooking is to have all ingredients ready to cook before turning on heat.

Chinese Chicken with Pea Pods

3 T. soy sauce
1 tsp. sherry flavoring
½ tsp. sugar
1 tsp. salt
pinch pepper
1 T. cornstarch
2 T. water
4 T. salad oil
pinch salt
1 small onion, finely chopped
1 clove garlic, finely chopped
¼ tsp. ginger, minced
1 1½-pound chicken, boned and cut into thin strips
1 8-ounce can bamboo shoots, drained
1 8-ounce can water chestnuts, drained and thinly sliced
1 6-ounce package frozen pea pods, thawed and dried

Combine the sauce mixture by blending together soy sauce, sherry flavoring, sugar, one teaspoon salt, and pepper.

Prepare the thickening by blending cornstarch with water.

Place a large skillet over high heat until a drop of water disappears almost immediately when flicked onto the pan. Add three tablespoons oil and pinch of salt; swirl the pan so that oil coats the surface. Add onion, garlic, and ginger to the pan and cook, stirring constantly and vigorously, until golden. Add chicken and cook, continuing to stir, for four minutes, or until light golden brown. Remove everything from the pan to a plate and keep warm.

Add remaining tablespoon of oil to skillet. Add bamboo shoots and water chestnuts, stirring rapidly for one minute. Add pea pods, stirring constantly, and cook for one more minute.

Return cooked chicken to the pan and add the sauce mixture. Stir and cook for one minute. Whisk the cornstarch mixture with a fork and add it to the pan, cooking and stirring for one minute more, or until the liquid is thickened and clear. Serve immediately.

4 to 6 servings
January 13, 1975

When you're especially busy–and who isn't?–an electric slow cooker can come to the rescue. A good meal to cook in it is:

Spanish Chicken

*1 3- to 4-pound chicken, cut in serving
  pieces
salt, pepper, paprika, to taste
garlic salt (optional)
1 6-ounce can tomato paste
¾ cup beer
1 small jar stuffed olives with liquid
  (¾ cup)
hot cooked rice or noodles, as needed*

Season chicken with salt, pepper, paprika, and garlic salt. Place in slow cooker. Mix tomato paste and beer together and pour over chicken. Add olives. Cover and cook on low 7 to 9 hours.
　　Serve over rice or noodles.
4 to 6 servings
November 27, 1976

Another good and convenient recipe for the electric slow-cooker.

California Chicken

*1 3-pound chicken, quartered
1 cup orange juice
½ cup chili sauce
2 T. soy sauce
1 T. molasses
1 tsp. dry mustard
1 tsp. garlic salt
2 T. green pepper, chopped
3 medium oranges, sliced into half
  cartwheels or 1 (13½-ounce) can
  mandarin oranges, drained*

Arrange chicken in pot. Combine orange juice, chili sauce, soy sauce, molasses, dry mustard, and garlic salt. Pour over chicken. Cover and cook on low eight to nine hours. Add green pepper and oranges 30 minutes before serving.
4 servings
January 1, 1977

Here's a good recipe for cooking chicken outdoors.

Chicken in the Skillet

*1 pound chicken breasts, drumsticks,
  thighs, or wings
2 slices bacon
½ cup onion, sliced
1 can condensed tomato soup
½ soup can water
¼ tsp. lemon rind, grated
2 T. lemon juice
1 T. brown sugar
1 tsp. prepared mustard
1 tsp. Worcestershire sauce
1 4-ounce can mushrooms, drained*

Prepare outdoor barbecue grill.
　　Cook bacon; remove from skillet and crumble. Place chicken in skillet; sprinkle with a little salt. Combine bacon with remaining ingredients and pour over chicken. Cover pan with aluminum foil.
　　Place on rack about five inches above bed of hot coals. Cook about 30 minutes. Turn chicken now and then, spooning sauce over. Uncover and continue to cook for 15 minutes, or until chicken is tender and sauce is thickened.
4 to 6 servings
June 21, 1958

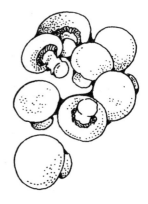

Another good and easy dish for the barbecue.

Butter-grilled Chicken Breasts

½ cup butter
¼ cup green onions, finely chopped
1 tsp. salt
⅛ tsp. pepper
¼ cup lemon juice
4 chicken breasts, halved (about 3
    pounds)

Melt butter in saucepan. Add onions, salt, and pepper; cook gently for three minutes. Remove from heat, add lemon juice. Place chicken in bowl and cover with sauce. Let stand, turning occasionally, while charcoal is heating.

When coals are white-hot, brush grill with fat and arrange six inches from coals. Place chicken breasts on grill, skin side up, and brush with remaining sauce. Grill about 30 to 50 minutes, turning every ten minutes until chicken is thoroughly done. After each turn, brush with remaining sauce.
6 servings
September 4, 1971

A unique and delicious recipe to cook over an outdoor grill.

Hawaiian Chicken

6 whole chicken breasts
½ cup vegetable oil
⅓ cup soy sauce
3 medium cloves garlic, minced
1 cup onion, finely chopped
3 T. light brown sugar, firmly packed
6 T. lemon juice
½ cup celery, chopped
1 tsp. salt
½ tsp. ground black pepper
½ cup toasted almonds, slivered
1 can (8 ounces) crushed pineapple,
    drained
1 package (8 ounces) pitted dates
6 lemon spirals

Place chicken breasts in large bowl. Combine one-quarter cup oil, soy sauce, garlic, one-half cup onion, sugar, and three tablespoons lemon juice. Pour over chicken; cover and marinate overnight.

In skillet, heat remaining oil; add remaining onion and celery; saute until golden. Stir in next four ingredients and remaining lemon juice. Reserve twelve pitted dates; cut remainder into quarters and stir into pineapple mixture.

Remove chicken from marinade. Fill each chicken breast with stuffing, about one-half cup. Secure closed with small metal skewers.

Grill over hot coals about 15 to 20 minutes on each side; baste with remaining marinade.

To serve, garnish with lemon spirals and reserved dates.
8 servings
May 28, 1977

New Orleans Barbecued Chicken

1 medium-sized onion, chopped
2 T. butter or margarine
1 bottle (14 ounces) tomato catsup
½ cup water
¼ cup molasses
1 tsp. prepared mustard
⅛ tsp. garlic salt
2 2½-pound chickens, quartered
¼ cup butter or margarine, melted
salt and pepper, to taste

Prepare barbecue grill; adjust grill three inches from coals.

Saute onion in two tablespoons butter or margarine until golden; stir in catsup, water, molasses, mustard, and garlic salt; simmer 15 minutes. Brush each chicken quarter with the melted butter. Arrange on grill, skin side up.

Grill 15 to 20 minutes, basting several times with sauce. Turn; grill 15 to 20 minutes longer, basting several times with sauce. Season with salt and pepper.
6 servings
June 17, 1967

Oven-Crusted Chicken

½ cup butter or margarine, melted
⅓ cup all-purpose flour
1½ tsp. salt
⅛ tsp. powdered thyme
⅛ tsp. dried rosemary, crushed
⅛ tsp. dried summer savory, crushed
1 frying chicken (1½- to 2-pounds),
* cut in serving pieces*
3 cups bite-size toasted corn biscuit
* cereal, crushed to 1¼ cups*

Preheat oven to 400 degrees.

Combine butter, flour, salt, thyme, rosemary, and savory. Dip chicken pieces first in butter mixture, then in cereal crumbs. Place on shallow baking sheet.

Bake in oven for 30 minutes. Turn pieces. Bake 25 minutes longer, or until crisp and brown.

Serve hot with gravy, if desired.

Gravy:

2 chicken bouillon cubes
2 cups warm water
¼ cup butter or margarine
¼ cup all-purpose flour

Dissolve bouillon cubes in water. Melt butter in saucepan; stir in flour until smooth. Add bouillon. Heat.
4 servings
June 17, 1967

2

Froning Cries Fowl!

Would you like to serve chicken that costs less and has a more delicious and intense flavor? It's easy, and G. W. Froning from the University of Nebraska would be delighted to tell you how—and he can do it in one word.

"Fowl!"

Let him explain.

"Fowl," he explains, "are mature chickens that were grown for egg production rather than for meat. They're usually at least a year and a half older than the chickens sold as broilers or fryers, and you can find them in the markets under the name 'stewing chickens,' or 'spent hens,' or 'mature chicken.'"

Fowl has an important advantage in that it's always more flavorful than the younger broilers and fryers. "The reason," Froning says, "is that older birds have had a chance to develop more of the flavor compounds that give chicken its characteristic taste."

Flavor chemistry is a complex subject, he further explains. Young birds may have the same flavor as fowl, but even so we don't perceive that flavor as being quite the same because it's much less intense.

The actual chicken flavor comes from sulfide-type compounds that increase in number as a chicken ages. Broilers and fryers don't have a chance

to develop their full potential of these flavor compounds since they are sent to market when they're only seven to eight weeks old. Fowl, on the other hand, will not reach the market before 18 months, and the birds may be considerably older yet. During that extra year and a half or more, their flavor components are increasing in number and that means a more flavorful bird for us.

Soup manufacturers know this, as do the baby food companies. You can be almost sure, when you buy a can of chicken soup or baby food, that the processor chose older birds for his product.

Unfortunately, as the bird ages, it also gets tougher. But as far as price goes, that toughness is an advantage because it's the reason stewing chicken costs less in the supermarket.

While it's true that these birds will be tougher, it's also true that if you cook them correctly, you can easily tenderize them. "Correct cooking for older birds," points out Froning, "means using moist heat. Try fowl in stews, fricassees, pot pies, or soups. But don't expect tender results if you broil or fry them—unless you tenderize them first by precooking them."

Froning has another, more technical, point on selecting the right bird. There are two major breeds of chickens: those used for laying eggs and those used for meat. The hens that lay eggs that will grow into meat chickens are usually better for home cooking than the hens that were laying eggs for human consumption. If you were to see a hen from a laying flock side by side with a hen from a broiler breeder flock, the difference would be as obvious as the difference between Twiggy and Marilyn Monroe.

His point is, if you ever have a choice, try for fowl that comes from a flock that's producing broilers in preference to one that's grown for laying eggs.

And what about cooking the two kinds? "In either case," says Froning, "the secret for tender, flavorful, and juicy fowl, is long and slow cooking. Stewing hens may be cooked by simmering or stewing in liquid in a covered pot until tender, usually about one and one-half hours to two hours. Laying hens—the Twiggies—require longer times, usually about two to three hours. The new slow cookers or crock pots are ideal for cooking fowl meat."

So, next time you're in the mood for chicken, try fowl. As you will discover when you try the recipes that follow, you will be rewarded with great taste at a bargain price.

Note to the reader: Any of the recipes in the previous chapter that call for cooked chicken can easily substitute fowl.

To cook an old fowl, put a pint or two of milk into the water that the fowl is to be boiled in. It gives a flavor to the meat and makes it white and juicy and gives the appearance of a young fowl. It is worth trying.
Wallaces Farmer, March 30, 1900

Menu for Curry Dinner, American-Style

Ceylon Curried Chicken*
Hot Rice
Toasted and Grated Coconut
Sliced Hard-Cooked Eggs
Pickled Onions
Peanuts
Pineapple Chunks
Bananas
Cranberry Chutney*
Creamy Buttermilk Sherbet*

There is almost no end to the condiments which may be included to complete the exotic flavor of curried chicken. The accompaniments really make the meal, and they may be few or many and may be added to the sauce or served separately. Use any—or all—of the items in this menu, served in small bowls accompanied by a large bowl of hot rice and the curried chicken.

Ceylon Curried Chicken

1 fowl, cut into serving pieces
½ onion, sliced
3 T. fat
3 T. all-purpose flour
1 tsp. (or more, to taste) curry powder
2 cups cooking broth
salt, to taste

Cover fowl with cold, salted water. Simmer three to three and one-half hours, or until tender. Remove meat from bones in as large pieces as possible. Skim fat from broth.

Cook onion in fat until tender. Add flour and curry powder. Slowly add one cup of the broth, cooled. Cook until smooth and thick, stirring constantly. Season with salt. Add chicken.

Serve hot on plates, along with rice and some of the condiments mentioned above.
4 to 6 servings
July 1, 1950

Cranberry Chutney

2 cups (1 pound can) whole cranberry
    sauce
2 T. light brown sugar
1 T. vinegar
¼ cup seedless raisins
¼ cup almonds, finely chopped
¼ tsp. garlic salt
¼ tsp. ginger
⅛ tsp. red pepper

Combine all ingredients. Chill thoroughly
to blend flavors.
Yield: 1 pint
January 16, 1960

Creamy Buttermilk Sherbet

3 eggs
¾ cup sugar
½ cup light corn syrup
2 cups buttermilk
⅓ cup lemon juice
2 T. grated lemon rind
strawberry sauce or preserves, as
    needed for topping

Beat eggs until foamy; gradually add sugar
and continue beating until thick. Fold in
corn syrup, buttermilk, lemon juice, and
lemon rind. Turn mixture into a refrigerator tray.

Freeze until amost firm. Turn into a
chilled mixing bowl and whip at high speed
with an electric mixer until creamy, about
four minutes. Pour into a one-quart mold
and freeze until firm.

To serve, unmold by turning upside
down on a platter and wrapping with a
warm towel for a few seconds. Spoon strawberry sauce or preserves over individual
servings.
8 servings
July 5, 1958

Chicken in Paprika Cream

1 5-pound fowl, cut in serving pieces
salt and pepper, to taste
4 T. butter
½-pound onions, finely chopped
1 T. paprika
1 cup tomato paste
2 cups sour cream
chicken stock, if needed to thin
    sauce

Season fowl with salt and pepper. Melt butter in saucepan and fry onions and paprika
for a few minutes until light yellow. Add
tomato paste and simmer for a few minutes.
Add sour cream. Place fowl in a deep baking dish. Add sauce and cover.

Bake in 350 degree oven for two hours
or more. Shake occasionally.

To serve, strain sauce and pour over bird.
If sauce is too thick, add a little stock.
4 to 6 servings
June 16, 1945

White Soup

Use a three or four pound fowl, three quarts
cold water, one tablespoonful salt, six pep-
percorns, one tablespoonful chopped
onions, two tablespoonfuls chopped celery,
one pint cream, one tablespoonful butter,
one tablespoonful corn starch, one
tablespoonful salt, one saltspoon white pepper, two eggs. Singe, clean, and wipe the
fowl. Cut off the legs and wings, and dis-
joint the body. Put it on to boil in cold
water. Let it come to a boil quickly, and
skim thoroughly. The meat may be
removed when tender, and the bones put
on to boil again. (Use the meat for cro-
quettes or other made dishes.) Add the salt
and vegetables. Simmer until reduced one-
half. Strain, and when cool remove the fat.
For one quart of stock allow one pint of
cream or milk. If cream, use a little less
flour for thickening. Boil the stock; add the
butter and flour, cooked together, and the
seasoning. Strain it over the eggs, stirring
as you pour, or the eggs will curdle.
December 12, 1901

Several Ways of Cooking Chicken

Boiling: An old chicken is best for boiling. Put a quart of water into a kettle and when it boils, put in a cleaned and trussed fowl. Add a large onion with half a dozen cloves stuck in it, a bay leaf, a bunch of sweet herbs, and a little salt and pepper. When done, lift out and drain carefully. Strain the broth in the kettle, thicken with flour, add a tablespoonful of chopped parsley and any other seasoning liked, pour over the chicken and serve at once.

Stuffed: Boil small onions in milk till nearly tender, and stuff a cleaned chicken with them. Boil, add minced boiled onions to the sauce, pour over chicken, sprinkle with chopped parsley, and serve at once.

With Rice: Prepare for boiling and boil for fifteen minutes. Then add an onion stuck with six cloves, pepper and salt, and a bunch of sweet herbs. When the onion is cooked to pieces, take it out and add a cupful of well-washed rice. Cook till the rice is tender, and pour rice around the chicken.
September 17, 1903

Rissoles

These make a tasty dish. Roll out some nice light paste, and have ready this mixture: Cold fowl, cold roast veal, and a little boiled ham (and meat scraps), all finely minced and seasoned well with pepper and salt. Mix well together with the beaten yolk of a raw egg and a spoonful of cream. Lay the mixture upon the paste in spoonfuls, and cover it over. The paste may be cut in any shape, then glazed with beaten egg, and fried in boiling lard to a golden brown color. Drain upon kitchen paper, store in writing paper, then put into boxes. They are nicest when hot, but will only require to be set in the oven for a few minutes. If the paste is rich they are as good cold as hot.
March 3, 1904

Chicken Soup

Remove the fat from one quart of water in which a chicken has been boiled. Season highly with salt, pepper and celery salt and a little onion if desired, and place to boil. Mash the yolks of three hard boiled eggs fine and mix them with half a cup of bread or cracker crumbs that have been soaked until soft in just sufficient milk. Chop the white meat of a chicken until fine like meal and stir it into the egg and bread paste. Add a pint of hot cream slowly and then rub all into the hot chicken liquor. Boil five minutes and add more salt if needed, and if too thick add more cream, or not thick enough add more fine cracker dust. It should be of the consistency of puree.
November 18, 1904

Scalloped Chicken, 1905

Take the dark meat of a boiled chicken, free from bones, skin and gristle; chop it in medium sized pieces, then take a quantity of boiled rice or macaroni and the same quantity of tomato sauce. Put in layers in a bake dish and cover with buttered crumbs. Bake till brown.
January 12, 1905

Jellied Chicken

A cold chicken in the form of jellied chicken makes a good supper dish. Put an ounce of gelatin in a pint of warm water on the back of the stove, and occasionally stir until it is dissolved. Then add a pint of chicken broth or bouillion to it and a high seasoning of salt and pepper. While the gelatin is being dissolved cut all the chicken off the bones. Place the meat in an earthen mold. Pour over the chicken the broth and gelatin, straining first. Press the meat down and let the broth cover it completely. Place a weight over it, and when the chicken is thoroughly jellied turn out of the mold and serve in thin slices.
February 22, 1906

Cooks in the early years of the century were thrifty with chicken. From 1905 we find this advice: "By following these two recipes we get from one chicken enough for two meals and when we tire of our fries, roasts, etc., this will be a welcome change."

And in its entirety, a recipe for Chicken Stew from 1911.

Chicken Stew

To the gravy of a fat hen add finely chopped potatoes and drop dumplings. Serve the whole on a large platter, putting the chicken in the middle and arranging the dumplings around the edge.
September 28, 1911

Chicken and Tomato Soup

Melt a tablespoonful of butter in a saucepan and add half an onion and two sprigs of parsley, chopped fine; stir and cook until yellowed, but not browned, then add a can of tomatoes and about three pints of chicken broth, and let simmer twenty minutes; press through a sieve and reheat to the boiling point; stir two tablespoonfuls of corn starch with water to pour and cook in the hot soup ten minutes; skim, if needed, season with salt and pepper and serve.
October 22, 1908

Creamed Fowl

This may be made from the scraps left over, or the undesirable pieces may be stewed and minced. For a pint of meat, heat one cupful of milk and thicken with one tablespoonful butter and flour. Season with salt and pepper and add the minced meat. When very hot, pour in the center of a dish and place mashed potatoes around the edge. If preferable, serve on toast. The latter is especially nice for supper.
January 29, 1914

Chicken with Ham Rolls

1 stewing chicken, 4 to 5 pounds,
 cut up
1 tsp. salt
1 large onion stuck with 6 cloves
2 stalks celery with leaves, sliced
4 T. butter
4 T. all-purpose flour
½ tsp. salt
1 cup light cream
¼ tsp. rosemary
2 cups soft bread crumbs
¼ cup onion, minced
2 T. parsley, minced
1 tsp. poultry seasoning
¼ tsp. salt
few grains pepper
8 thin slices cooked ham

Place chicken in large saucepan. Add one teaspoon salt, onion with cloves, celery, and enough water to barely cover. Bring to boil. Cover and simmer one and one-half hours or until chicken is tender. Cook giblets separately, drain and chop. Cool chicken in broth. Remove chicken; discard bones and skin, keeping pieces of meat as large as possible. Arrange chicken in large shallow casserole. Strain broth; reserve.

Melt butter. Blend in flour and one-half teaspoon salt. Add two cups of broth and cream. Stir over medium heat until smooth and thickened. Add rosemary and chopped giblets. Cook over low heat 10 minutes longer. Pour over chicken.

Combine bread crumbs, minced onion, parsley, poultry seasoning, remaining salt, and pepper. Add enough of remaining broth to hold ingredients together, one-third to one-half cup. Spoon equal amount in center of each slice of ham, reserving about two tablespoons. Roll ham around stuffing. Place rolls in casserole on top of chicken. Sprinkle with reserved stuffing.

Bake in 350 degree oven for 30 minutes.
8 servings
May 2, 1970

Down South Stew

1 stewing chicken, cut up
2½ to 3 quarts water
4 tsp. salt
1 small onion, chopped
2 cups corn
1 cup cooked tomatoes
2 tsp. salt
⅛ tsp. pepper
1 tsp. Worcestershire sauce
6 ounces elbow spaghetti
1 cup cooked okra

Place chicken in a large saucepot and add enough water to cover. Add salt and onion. Bring to a boil, reduce heat, cover, and simmer until tender, about one hour and 45 minutes.

Remove chicken from broth and cool. Then remove all but two quarts of broth; if necessary, skim excess fat from surface. Add corn, tomatoes, salt, pepper, and Worcestershire. Cook about 15 minutes, stirring occasionally. Add spaghetti and cook 10 minutes longer.

Meanwhile, remove chicken from bones and cut into pieces. Add chicken and okra to stew and cook just long enough to heat thoroughly.
6 servings
February 21, 1959

Chicken Cacciatore

1 4- to 5-pound roasting chicken, cut
into serving pieces
½ cup all-purpose flour
3 tsp. salt
1 tsp. paprika
½ tsp. thyme or oregano
¼ tsp. black pepper
2 cups stewed tomatoes
½ cup green pepper, chopped
½ cup onion, chopped
½ cup celery, chopped
1 clove garlic, mashed
1 T. Worcestershire sauce
½ cup mushroom stems and pieces
Parmesan cheese, as desired

Melt fat from the chicken in a skillet or Dutch oven. Combine flour, salt, paprika, thyme, and black pepper; roll chicken pieces in the mixture and coat evenly. Brown pieces thoroughly in the fat.

Combine the tomatoes, green pepper, onion, celery, garlic, Worcestershire sauce, and any liquid from the mushrooms; heat for five minutes. Pour over the chicken. Cover, and simmer two and one-half hours, or until the chicken is fork-tender. Spoon sauce over the chicken two or three times while cooking.

To serve, place chicken on a platter. Stir mushrooms into sauce and boil to blend. Pour over chicken and sprinkle with cheese.
6 servings
May 3, 1958

Scalloped Chicken

1 2½- to 3-pound stewing chicken
⅓ cup (⅔ stick) butter
2 T. onion, chopped
⅓ cup all-purpose flour
1 tsp. salt
1½ cups chicken broth
2 eggs, separated
1 cup milk
1 cup bread crumbs, reserving a few
*   for topping*
paprika, as desired

Sauce:

1 cup mushrooms, sliced
¼ cup pimiento olives, sliced
¼ cup (½ stick) butter

Remove neck and giblets. Place chicken (whole or cut into serving pieces) in a Dutch oven. Add just enough water to cover. Cook until tender, two and a half to three hours. Remove chicken from broth. Cool and remove meat from bones. Skim fat from broth.

Melt butter in saucepan. Add onions and saute until tender. Stir in flour and salt to form paste. Add broth gradually. Cook mixture over moderate heat, stirring constantly until thickened and smooth. Beat egg yolks in medium-sized mixing bowl. Add milk and thickened broth to egg yolks. Stir in bread crumbs. Beat egg whites until stiff but not dry. Fold into cooled broth mixture. Place three cups cooked chicken in shallow casserole. Pour sauce over chicken. Sprinkle top with bread crumbs, if desired. Sprinkle with paprika.

Bake in 350 degree oven for 50 minutes.

Meanwhile, prepare additional sauce by sauteing mushrooms and olives in butter about 10 minutes.

To serve, cut casserole into serving portions and top with mushroom-olive sauce.
6 servings
April 22, 1977

Hot Chicken Loaf

1 4-pound stewing chicken
2 tsp. salt
4 cups cooked rice
1 tsp. salt
¼ cup pimiento, chopped
1 tsp. paprika
4 eggs, beaten
¼ cup chicken fat, skimmed from
*   broth*
2 cups chicken broth
1 cup milk

Cook chicken in water to cover with two teaspoons salt. Pour broth into containers. Cool quickly and refrigerate. Remove meat from bones, cutting into one-inch cubes. Combine chicken, rice, one teaspoon salt, pimiento, paprika, eggs, chicken fat, two cups broth, and milk. Stir to blend well.

Prepare mold: use a two-quart ring mold, large bread-loaf pan, or heart shaped pans. Brush inside well with melted butter. Pack chicken-rice mixture into pan.

Bake in 350 degree oven for one hour. Let loaf stay in pan 10 minutes to steam. Loosen edges before removing to platter.
6 servings
May 17, 1958

3

Talking Turkey

Jim Cunningham is afraid of low flying jets. And planes. And worst of all—helicopters.

But his fear is not your usual garden-variety paranoia. If low flying aircraft give him the willies, it's for good reason. If you were a turkey grower like him, you'd feel the same way.

To find out why, let's visit him in his "grow-out" barns in Merced, California. He's standing inside one of the 500-foot long turkey barns, surrounded by about 7,000 twenty-pound birds. There's a low and continuous "gobble, gobble" sound in the background as Cunningham speaks.

"All turkey growers dislike low-flying aircraft of any kind," he explains. "That's because turkeys panic when things fly over them. They're genetically wired to fear hawks or eagles, and they can't distinguish between a plane and a hawk."

"What happens," we ask, "when an airplane does fly low overhead?"

"I've had it happen," he answers, "and it's awful." He makes a sweeping, whooshing gesture with both hands as if indicating a dam bursting. "The birds panic and try to escape. Waves and waves of them pour against the walls and fences until they break them."

We look at the 7,000 birds that are eyeing us and try to imagine herding them back into the barn if they had

escaped. And the problem wouldn't stop with just these birds. Nearby, Cunningham has seven other flocks of 9,000 each. If we were faced with recapturing that many winged creatures every time an airplane spooked them, we'd feel nervous about low flying aircraft too.

Fortunately, this doesn't happen often and Cunningham rarely loses birds. This is important to him, not only economically since they're his living, but also because he likes turkeys and he believes in his product.

"We're an industry that responds to consumer needs and wants. For instance, a generation ago, a family Thanksgiving might mean four generations and enough guests to finish off a 30-pound turkey. Today, with smaller families, we market birds that are half that size."

A generation or so ago, you had to buy a tom turkey to get a large bird. Toms got bigger than hens, but at the same time they got old and they got tough. Today, turkey breeders have succeeded in breeding turkeys that reach market weight long before they get old and tough. There's no discernible difference either in flavor or tenderness between a tom and a hen—the only difference that matters is that the hens are usually around 10 to 14 pounds, while the toms are 16 to 24 pounds.

"Buy according to the size that fits your needs, and don't be concerned about sex," is Cunningham's recommendation. "What about frozen versus fresh?" we ask.

"Turkey is a meat that feezes exceptionally well," he answers. "Taste panelists say that there is little difference in quality between a fresh bird and a frozen one. The big difference is in cost. To have fresh turkey at holiday times, the processing plants have to double their shifts and pay overtime as well, and this adds to the costs. If you find there's not much difference in the price of the fresh bird, buy it, but if there's a big difference, then go for the frozen."

But what about other ways of buying turkey—the alternatives to going for a whole bird? Henry Turner from the California Turkey Federation suggests that small families take advantage of a recent innovation in the turkey industry, the practice of selling turkey pieces, such as thighs or drumsticks or breasts or hams. "And consumers who try the new turkey products—ground turkey, turkey salami, turkey pastrami—love them," exclaims Turner. "These products are all highly nutritional, easily digested, and they're great for older people because they're high in protein yet have little fat."

Turner has some advice for us on the matter of cooking the bird: "If your old cookbooks or meat thermometers say you need to cook turkey to an internal temperature of 185 degrees, please ignore what you read! The ideal temperature for moist, tender, juicy turkey is just under 180 degrees." He goes on, "In fact, roasting a turkey is as simple as one, two three." And to make it simple for you, here is the National Turkey Federation's method for roasting the bird:

Roast Turkey

1 Thaw: Leave the turkey in its original bag and place on a refrigerator tray (takes 3 to 4 days to defrost), or place on a tray at room temperature in a closed grocery bag (it'll take about an hour a pound to defrost). If you're in a real hurry, you can cover the turkey—still in its original wrapping—with cold water, changing the water occasionally (takes 30 minutes a pound to defrost).

2 Prepare for the oven: Remove the neck and giblets from the cavities. Rinse the bird and pat it dry. (You can cook the giblets and neck for broth and dressing while the bird is roasting.) Rub salt generously in the cavities, and, if desired, insert pieces of celery, carrots, onion, and parsley for added flavor. Fasten down legs by tying or tucking under skin band and skewer neck skin to back, and twist wings akimbo under bird. Place the bird on a rack in a shallow roasting pan, breast side up. Brush with butter, and if a roasting thermometer is used, insert it into the thick part of the thigh. The bulb must not touch the bone.

3 Roast: Roast in a preheated 325 degree oven to just under 180 degrees, or about four hours for a 12 pound bird, five hours for a 16 pounder, and six hours for a 20 pound bird. You can tell if the turkey is done when the thick part of the drumstick feels soft when pressed with the thumb and forefinger and the drumstick and thigh move easily.

You can cook your favorite stuffing in a dish alongside the turkey.

When the meal is over, hope that you have lots of turkey meat left over to use in some of the recipes that follow. Or if you don't want to begin with a whole roast bird, look for the turkey parts you can buy today in the meat section of your supermarket.

Menu for Thanksgiving Dinner

Roast Turkey
Nut Stuffing*
Spicy Cranberry Sauce*
Sweet Potatoes in Orange Cups*
Green Beans
Celery Sticks
Cranberry Muffin Gobblers* and Butter
Celery Sticks
Deluxe Pumpkin Pie*
Turkey Cookies*
Milk
Coffee or Tea

*Recipe Included

Nut Stuffing

½ cup butter
½ cup onion, chopped
2 cups Brazil nuts or toasted almonds, chopped
¼ cup parsley, chopped
1 cup celery, chopped including leaves
2 tsp. salt
¼ tsp. pepper
1 tsp. poultry seasoning
8 cups soft bread cubes
2 eggs, beaten
1 cup stock or water

Melt butter in large saucepan or skillet; add onion and cook over low heat until onion is tender, but not brown. Stir in nuts, parsley, celery, salt, pepper, and poultry seasoning; add bread cubes and toss lightly. Remove from heat; stir in eggs and stock. Stuffing for one 12-pound turkey
November 21, 1964

66

Spicy Cranberry Sauce

1 cup water
1¼ cups light brown sugar
¾ cup white sugar
½ cup vinegar
2 tsp. whole cloves
2 cinnamon sticks
1 pound (4 cups) cranberries

Place water, brown sugar, white sugar, vinegar, cloves, and cinnamon in saucepan. Bring to a boil and boil rapidly for five minutes. Strain. Add cranberries and cook slowly until cranberries pop open, about 15 minutes. Cool, then chill.
Yield: 1 quart
November 16, 1963

Sweet Potatoes in Orange Cups

6 to 8 medium sweet potatoes, washed
8 to 10 medium oranges
¼ cup butter or margarine
½ cup brown sugar
½ tsp. salt
¼ cup orange juice
marshmallows, as needed

Preheat oven to 375 degrees.

Cook potatoes in one inch of boiling, salted water or bake in 350 degree oven until tender when tested with a fork. Cut a slice off the stem end of each orange. With a small sharp knife, cut around inside edge of oranges to loosen pulp. With fingers and a spoon, remove pulp and juice, being careful not to break shells. Press juice from pulp and reserve. Notch shells, if desired. Drain boiled potatoes, peel, and mash. Add butter, sugar, salt and orange juice. Mix until blended. Spoon into orange shells. Top with marshmallows.

Bake in oven 15 to 20 minutes, or until marshmallows are golden and potatoes are hot.
4 to 5 servings
November 15, 1969

Cranberry Muffin Gobblers

1 cup fresh cranberries
⅓ cup sugar
2 cups all-purpose flour, sifted
3 tsp. baking powder
⅓ cup sugar
½ tsp. ground cinnamon
1 egg, slightly beaten
¾ cup milk
¼ cup (½ stick) butter or margarine,
melted
wooden picks
dark seedless raisins
golden seedless raisins
whole fresh cranberries

Preheat oven to 400 degrees.

Wash one cup cranberries thoroughly, removing all stems. Place in a small saucepan with one-third cup sugar. Cover and heat to boiling. Continue heating for another two or three minutes or until berries are soft and some have popped.

Sift flour, baking powder, sugar, and cinnamon together into bowl. Combine egg, milk, and butter. Add this liquid along with the cooked cranberries to the flour mixture. Stir just enough to mix ingredients. Fill well-oiled muffin tins about two-thirds full of batter.

Bake in oven for 25 minutes. Turn muffins out of tins immediately and place on a rack.

To make turkey tails, string wooden picks with four raisins, alternating dark and light. Top each with a whole, fresh cranberry. Place four raisin-cranberry picks side by side on the top edge of each muffin. To make the turkey heads, string three cranberries on a wooden pick. Push into muffin on opposite side of tail.

18 muffin gobblers
November 17, 1973

Deluxe Pumpkin Pie

Here's something new in pumpkin pie. A top garnish of grated sharp cheese and tiny slivers of candied ginger make this pie something extra special. Part of the pumpkin will be used for the pie filling and the remainder may be baked in custard cups.

2 large eggs
¾ cup sugar
½ tsp. ginger
½ tsp. nutmeg
½ tsp. ground cloves
½ tsp. salt
1¾ cups canned pumpkin
1½ cups milk
pastry for one-crust 9-inch pie
¼ pound sharp cheese
candied ginger, slivered, as needed

Preheat oven to 450 degrees.

Beat eggs in mixing bowl. Add sugar, ginger, nutmeg, cloves, salt, and pumpkin. Mix well. Add milk and stir until mixture is smooth. Fill a pastry-lined nine-inch pie pan with pumpkin mixture.

Bake in oven for 10 minutes. Reduce heat to 350 degrees and continue to bake for about 45 minutes, or until the pumpkin mixture is firm and the crust is well browned.

Garnish with cheese and ginger.

1 9-inch pie
December 20, 1947

And finally, a special holiday favorite for the young—and young at heart.

Turkey Cookies

1 prepared batch of your favorite
* sugar cookie recipe*
1 turkey shaped cookie cutter
1 2-inch round scalloped cookie cutter
1 prepared recipe of confectionary
* sugar frosting*

Roll out the dough to one-eighth-inch thickness on a lightly floured board. Cut half the dough with turkey cookie cutter and remaining half with scalloped cutter. Make a dent with the edge of a saucer in the center of each scalloped cookie.

Bake in a 350 degree oven about 10 minutes. Remove from cookie sheet and cool.

Fill indentations with frosting. Stand turkey cookies upright in frosting.
Approximately 2 dozen cookies
November 15, 1952

Turkey Size Guide

When buying turkeys under 12 pounds, allow ¾ to 1 pound per serving. Allow ½ to ¾ pound per serving of medium or heavy birds, 12 pounds and over. Actual servings also depend on quality of turkey, method of cooking, and carving skill. In most instances large birds are more economical for use in future meals.

Turkey in pounds	Servings
6 to 8	6 to 10
8 to 12	10 to 20
12 to 16	20 to 32
16 to 20	32 to 40
20 to 24	40 to 50

Cranberry Relish

1 pound can jellied cranberry sauce
½ cup applesauce
¼ cup raisins
¼ tsp. cinnamon

Crush cranberry sauce with a fork. Stir in applesauce, raisins, and cinnamon. Chill for several hours.
November 15, 1969

Appetizers

Tiny Turkey Turnovers

1 cup cooked turkey livers, finely
* chopped*
6 slices fried bacon, crumbled
½ cup mayonnaise or salad dressing
1 T. onion, minced
2 T. cream or milk
1 T. prepared mustard
1 tsp. salt
1 tsp. monosodium glutamate
1 recipe plain pastry
1 egg, slightly beaten
1 T. water
all-purpose flour, as needed

Preheat oven to 425 degrees.

Combine turkey liver, bacon, mayonnaise, onion, cream, mustard, salt, and monosodium glutamate; blend well. Roll out pastry dough on lightly floured board and cut in three-inch rounds with scalloped cookie cutter. Place small spoonful of filling on each round of pastry; fold in half and pinch edges together tightly. Prick each turnover with fork and brush with glaze made from slightly beaten egg and water.

Place turnovers on cookie sheet and bake in oven for 10 to 15 minutes or until pastry is done. Serve warm.
Makes 18 turnovers
January 21, 1961

Turkey Teasers

2 cups cooked turkey, chopped
3 hard-cooked eggs, chopped
1 cup Cheddar cheese, grated
2 T. green pepper, chopped
2 T. onion, chopped
2 T. stuffed olives, chopped
½ cup mayonnaise or salad dressing
2 dozen miniature hamburger buns
parsley, if desired

Combine all ingredients except buns and blend well. Cut buns in half. Top each with tablespoonful of turkey mixture.

Place on the broiler pan and broil six inches from heat for five minutes or until mixture bubbles and looks puffy. Top with sprig of parsley, if desired.

Serve hot as appetizers. This filling may be used hot or cold as regular sandwich filling.

48 appetizers
January 21, 1961

Here's a hearty snack that would be great at a winter party—or any time.

Toasted Turkey Appetizers

¼ cup onion, chopped
3 T. butter
3 T. all-purpose flour
1 tsp. salt
1 cup milk
1 tsp. Worcestershire sauce
2 cups cooked turkey, cubed
thinly sliced rye bread or crackers,
    as needed
sharp Cheddar cheese, as needed
cranberry sauce, as needed

Preheat oven to 425 degrees.

Cook onions in butter until golden brown. Stir in flour and salt. Add milk. Continue to cook, stirring until thick. Stir in Worcestershire sauce and turkey. Mix well to combine flavors.

To serve, spread one teaspoon of the mixture on bread or crackers. Top with cheese. Place on a cookie sheet and toast in oven for three to five minutes, or just until cheese melts.

Serve hot, garnished with cranberry sauce.

October 17, 1959

Soups

Turkey Gobbler Soup

2 cups tomatoes
½ cup celery, chopped
1 onion, chopped
2 chicken bouillon cubes
¼ tsp. pepper
4 T. butter
¼ cup all-purpose flour
4 cups milk
1 tsp. salt
1½ cups cooked turkey, diced

In a saucepan cook tomatoes, celery, onion, bouillon cubes, and pepper for about 15 minutes. In another pan melt butter over low heat. Blend in flour. Add milk, stirring constantly. Cook until smooth and thickened. Season with salt. Add vegetable mixture and turkey. Heat to serving temperature.

5 to 6 servings
November 22, 1969 (Courtesy of the National Dairy Council)

Curried Turkey Soup

1 cup celery, diced
1 cup apple, peeled and diced
½ cup onion, chopped
4 T. butter
¼ cup all-purpose flour
2 tsp. curry powder
1½ tsp. salt
⅛ tsp. pepper
4 cups milk
2 cups cooked turkey (or chicken), diced

Saute celery, apple, and onion in butter until apple and onion are tender but not brown. Blend in flour, curry powder, salt, and pepper. Add milk, stirring constantly until thickened. Add turkey. Heat to serving temperature.

6 servings
December, 1972

When you are in a hurry and want a good and hearty meal that is convenient to prepare, try:

Golden Turkey Chowder

½ cup onion, chopped
1 clove garlic, minced
1 tsp. basil leaves, crushed
2 T. butter
2 cans mushroom soup
2 soup cans water
1 16-oz. can stewed tomatoes, cut up
2 cups cooked turkey, diced
1½ cups medium noodles, uncooked

Saute onion and garlic with basil in butter until tender. Stir in soup and water; add tomatoes, turkey, and noodles. Bring to a boil, then reduce heat. Cook 10 minutes or until noodles are done, stirring occasionally.
4 to 6 servings
November 19, 1977

Turkey Chowder

2 slices bacon, chopped
¼ cup onion, chopped
1 cup celery, diced
2 cups potatoes, cubed
1 cup cooked turkey, diced
2 cups turkey broth
1 cup corn
2 T. parsley, chopped
2 T. all-purpose flour
1 cup milk
salt and pepper, to taste

Place bacon in frying pan over low heat. When partially cooked, add onion. Continue cooking until onion is soft and bacon is brown. In a saucepan, cook celery, potatoes, and turkey in broth until vegetables are tender. Then add corn, cooked bacon and onion, and parsley. Blend flour with milk and stir into cooking mixture. Cook about 15 minutes, stirring occasionally. Season with salt and pepper.
6 servings
January 5, 1963

Herbed Turkey Stew with Tomato Dumplings

Tomato Dumplings:
1 cup sifted all-purpose flour
½ tsp. salt
1½ tsp. baking powder
¼ tsp. poultry seasoning
½ cup tomato juice

Sift flour with salt, baking powder, and poultry seasoning. Stir in tomato juice, mixing only until ingredients are blended.

Stew:
3 cups turkey stock
6 carrots, quartered
3 potatoes, quartered
½ cup celery, diced
½ cup green peas
2 cups cooked turkey, diced
1 tsp. poultry seasoning
1 tsp. salt
⅛ tsp. pepper
3 T. all-purpose flour
3 T. cold water

Bring turkey stock to boiling point in a 5-quart saucepan. Add carrots, potatoes, celery, and green peas. Cover and cook until crisp-tender. Add turkey, poultry seasoning, salt, and pepper; mix well. Mix flour with cold water to make a paste. Stir into stew and heat to boiling point, stirring well.

Drop tomato dumpling mixture from a teaspoon over the top of the stew; cover and cook 12 minutes without lifting the lid. Serve at once.
6 servings
November 12, 1966

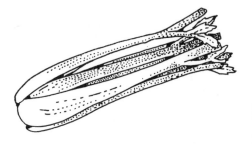

Turkey Stew with Herb Dumplings

Herb Dumplings:

1½ cups sifted all-purpose flour
2 tsp. baking powder
1 tsp. salt
3 T. parsley, finely chopped
⅛ tsp. poultry seasoning
1 egg
¾ cup milk

Sift together flour, baking powder, and salt. Stir in parsley and poultry seasoning. Beat egg and stir in milk; add to flour mixture and stir only until flour is moistened.

Turkey Stew:

4 T. butter
½ cup onion, chopped
1 cup celery, diced
2 cups carrots, cut in 1-inch pieces
1½ cups turkey stock
2 cups water
2 tsp. salt
1 cup green beans, cut in 1-inch
*   pieces*
1½ cups cooked turkey, diced
3 T. all-purpose flour
⅓ cup water
1 tsp. Worcestershire sauce

Melt butter in a 4- or 5-quart covered saucepan or Dutch oven. Add onion, celery, and carrots; cover and let simmer about 10 minutes. Add turkey stock, water, and salt. Cover and cook gently about 15 minutes, or until vegetables are tender. Add beans and turkey; continue cooking about 5 minutes longer. Blend flour and ⅓ cup water; stir into vegetable mixture with Worcestershire sauce. Bring to a boil; continue cooking for 5 minutes, stirring occasionally. Drop dumpling mixture by tablespoons on top of stew. Cover and steam 10 minutes. Uncover and continue cooking for 10 minutes longer.
4 servings with 12 dumplings
November 13, 1965

The Thanksgiving Dinner

Shall we have turkey for Thanksgiving dinner? To be sure, turkey will be on the Thanksgiving dinner table, tho it be only pictured turkey place cards. Since the day of the first Thanksgiving, when our forefathers ate wild turkey and gave thanks, the turkey has been the emblem of Thanksgiving Day.

Much of the turkey served in hotels on Thanksgiving Day is roast pork. Served with dressing and cranberry sauce, it is not easy to detect the difference.
Wallaces Farmer,
November 19, 1920

Butter Garnishes

Butter added to clear hot soups enhances the flavor and decorates. Try some of these easy tricks. Float butter balls rolled in parsley, chives, or grated cheese. . . . Top with butter pat capped with smidgen of shredded cheese. . . . Serve with butter ball rolled around a surprise filling of cheese square or toast cube. . . . Add butter seasoned with herbs or spices, then shaped into balls or pats. . . . Garnish with butter pat coated with minced nuts or crushed cereal. . . . Float butter pat topped with thin slice of radish.
Prairie Farmer, January 3, 1956

Sandwiches

Turkey Cranberry Sandwich

1 cup turkey (or chicken), diced
½ cup celery, diced
1 tsp. salt
⅓ cup mayonnaise
1 loaf unsliced bread
6 T. butter
⅔ cup cranberry jelly
4 packages (3-ounces each) cream
   cheese
¼ cup milk

Combine turkey, celery, salt, and mayonnaise. Using a sharp knife, remove crusts from top, sides, and ends of loaf of bread; cut into 4 lengthwise slices. Spread the first slice with 1½ tablespoons butter and ⅓ cup cranberry jelly. Spread second slice with another 1½ tablespoons butter and place on top of jellied layer buttered side down. Cover top of the slice with turkey mixture, over which place third slice of bread. Spread top with 1½ tablespoons butter and then with ⅓ cup cranberry jelly. Spread one side of remaining slice with rest of butter and place over cranberry layer, buttered side down. Soften cream cheese with milk. Spread over top and sides of the loaf. Chill until ready to serve.

Garnish as desired with cranberry jelly and slice to serve.
6 servings
December 5, 1959

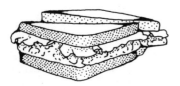

Turkey Vegetable Sandwich

1 medium cucumber, thinly sliced
½ cup Italian dressing
3 T. yogurt or sour cream
1 T. spicy brown mustard
12 slices bread
lettuce leaves
3 medium tomatoes, thinly sliced
6 slices cooked turkey (or chicken)

Marinate cucumber in Italian dressing for 30 minutes. Combine yogurt or sour cream and mustard. Spread on bread. Cover 6 slices with lettuce, tomatoes, cucumber, and turkey. Close with remaining bread.
6 servings
October 11, 1969

Orange Turkey Club Sandwich

8 slices bread
4 T. Thousand Island or Louis dressing
8 slices bacon, cooked
4 slices Swiss cheese
8 slices turkey meat (about 8 ounces)
2 oranges, peeled and thinly sliced
crisp lettuce leaves

Spread 4 slices of bread with dressing. Layer bacon, cheese, turkey, orange, and lettuce on each of the 4 slices. Top with remaining bread slices. Cut sandwiches in quarters and secure with wooden picks.
4 servings
June 23, 1973

Give canned turkey noodle soup an eastern touch by adding ¼ teaspoon curry powder to 1 can of soup thinned with an equal amount of milk. Heat and sprinkle with grated coconut before serving.
Prairie Farmer, July 15, 1961

Turkey Long Burgers

1½ cups cooked turkey, diced
1 cup Cheddar cheese, shredded
½ cup mayonnaise or salad dressing
2 T. onion, chopped
3 hard-cooked eggs, chopped
2 T. sweet pickle relish, drained
8 to 10 frankfurter buns, buttered

Combine turkey, cheese, mayonnaise, onion, eggs, and relish. Fill buns with mixture. Wrap each bun individually in foil.
   Bake in 350 degree oven for 25 to 30 minutes.
4 to 5 servings
November 13, 1971

Turkey Sandwich Supper

Potato Patties:
3 cups cooked potatoes, mashed
3 T. onion, chopped
2 egg yolks
coarse bread crumbs, as needed
butter, as needed

Sandwich:
8 slices cooked turkey
turkey gravy, as needed
4 slices bread

Combine potatoes, onion, and egg yolks. Shape into 8 patties. Coat with bread crumbs. Brown on both sides in butter. Meanwhile, heat turkey in gravy.
   Place hot turkey slices on the bread and pour remaining gravy over all. Serve with potato patties.
4 servings
November 24, 1973

A meal by itself.

Saucy Turkey Sandwiches

6 1-inch slices bread, toasted
12 slices cooked turkey breast
6 slices cooked ham
12 spears cooked broccoli
12 slices bacon, partially cooked
6 sprigs parsley (optional)
6 slices red apple, unpeeled
12 slices orange

Cheese sauce:
3 T. butter
3 T. all-purpose flour
1½ cups milk
1 cup American cheese, shredded

Prepare sauce: Melt butter; blend in flour to make a smooth paste. Add milk gradually, stirring constantly until thickened. Blend in cheese, stirring until smooth.
   Place bread in the bottom of individual casserole dishes. Cover each slice with two slices turkey, one slice ham, and two broccoli spears. Pour ½ cup cheese sauce over each dish. Place two slices bacon diagonally over cheese. Broil until bacon is completely cooked. Place parsley in center of each sandwich. Alternate two orange slices and one apple slice over each.
   Serve hot.
6 servings
November 21, 1964

A tasty, quick, and easy way to use those small chunks of cooked turkey that are leftover after the Big Day.

Turkey Sandwich Grill

Team equal amounts of chopped, cooked turkey (or chicken) and finely diced celery. Add sweet relish, salt, and pepper to taste, plus mayonnaise or salad dressing until spreadable. Spread on toast, sprinkle with grated Cheddar cheese. Place in a hot oven or broiler to melt cheese. Garnish with chili sauce.
January 22, 1972

Salads

When you need a main dish salad for a crowd, or an attractive addition to a buffet, try—

Molded Main Dish Salad

1 T. unflavored gelatin
¼ cup cold water
1½ cups hot chicken broth
2 cups cooked turkey (or chicken), diced
2 cups cooked rice
1½ cups celery, diced
1 tsp. salt
¼ tsp. white pepper
¼ cup green onions with tops, chopped
½ cup sour cream
½ cup mayonnaise
1 tsp. lemon juice
2 packages orange gelatin, 3-oz. each
2 cups hot orange juice
2 cups jellied cranberry sauce
salad greens, as needed

Soften unflavored gelatin in water. Dissolve in chicken broth. Chill until partly thickened. Add turkey, rice, celery, salt, pepper, green onions, sour cream, mayonnaise, and lemon juice. Mix well. Spoon into a loaf pan, and chill.

Blend together orange gelatin with orange juice and cranberry sauce. Chill until partly thickened. Pour over chicken mixture. Chill until firm.

To serve, unmold onto serving platter. Garnish with salad greens.
10 servings
June 24, 1972

And another molded main dish salad for a crowd.

Shimmering Turkey Mold

2 packages unflavored gelatin
4 cups highly seasoned turkey broth
2 T. lemon juice
5 cups cooked turkey, chopped
2 cups pineapple, chopped
3 hard-cooked eggs, sliced
salad greens, as needed

Sprinkle gelatin on one cup cold broth to soften. Heat remaining broth almost to boiling. Dissolve softened gelatin in hot broth. Cool to room temperature. Add lemon juice and season to taste. Chill mixture until it is the consistency of unbeaten egg white, then add turkey and pineapple. Pour into a mold and chill until firm.

To serve, unmold on a serving platter. Garnish with eggs and salad greens.
12 servings
February 16, 1963

Tangy Turkey Salad

2 cups cooked turkey, diced
2 cups celery, diced
½ cup jellied cranberry sauce
1 T. powdered sugar
⅓ cup prepared horseradish
½ tsp. salt
½ cup heavy cream, whipped
lettuce leaves, as needed

Chill turkey and celery for several hours. Crush cranberry with fork. Blend in sugar, horseradish, and salt. Chill. Just before serving fold cranberry mixture into whipped cream, then combine with turkey mixture. Serve on lettuce.
4 servings
November 18, 1961

Turkey and Kidney Bean Salad

1 cup cooked turkey, chopped
1¼ cups cooked kidney beans
⅓ cup sweet pickle, chopped
⅔ cup celery, chopped
1 T. onion, finely chopped
2 hard-cooked eggs, diced
1 tsp. salt
3 T. mayonnaise
1 tsp. prepared mustard
1 tsp. pickle juice

Combine all ingredients. Toss lightly. Chill for at least an hour to blend flavors.
6 servings
April 26, 1969

Polynesian Turkey Salad

4 cups cooked turkey, diced
1 5-oz. can water chestnuts, drained and sliced
1 cup celery, bias cut
¼ cup green onions, bias cut
¼ cup green pepper, chopped
2 hard-cooked eggs, chopped
1 tsp. salt
1 cup mayonnaise or salad dressing
¼ cup frozen orange juice concentrate, thawed
lettuce leaves, as needed
1 11-oz. can mandarin oranges, drained
½ cup toasted almonds, diced

In a large bowl combine turkey, water chestnuts, celery, green onions, green pepper, eggs, salt, mayonnaise or salad dressing, and orange juice. Chill.

To serve, mound salad mixture on lettuce leaves. Garnish with oranges and almonds.
6 to 8 servings
November 13, 1971

Turkey Fruit Salad

1½ cups cooked turkey, chopped
1 cup seedless green grapes
1 5-oz. can water chestnuts, drained and chopped
1 11-oz. can mandarin orange segments, drained
½ cup mayonnaise or salad dressing
½ tsp. salt
¼ tsp. curry powder
lettuce leaves, as needed
sliced toasted almonds, as desired (optional)

Combine turkey, grapes, water chestnuts, and orange segments. Mix together mayonnaise or salad dressing, salt, and curry powder. Toss with turkey mixture.

To serve, mound in bowl lined with lettuce leaves. May garnish with almonds.
3 to 4 servings
November 20, 1976

Turkey Macaroni Salad

1 T. salt
3 quarts boiling water
2 cups elbow macaroni
1 cup pecans
salt, as needed
1 tsp. butter
1 cup cottage cheese
1 T. sugar
½ tsp. paprika
¼ cup light cream
1 cup cooked turkey, diced
1½ cups peaches, sliced
crisp greens, as needed

Preheat oven to 350 degrees.

Add 1 tablespoon salt to rapidly boiling water. Gradually add macaroni so water continues to boil. Cook uncovered, stirring occasionally, until tender. Drain in colander; rinse with cold water, and drain again.

Sprinkle pecans with salt. Dot with butter. Bake in oven 20 minutes, stirring occasionally.

Combine cottage cheese, sugar, paprika, and cream. Toss cottage cheese mixture with macaroni, turkey, and peaches. Chill.

To serve, mix in pecans and mound on greens.
4 to 6 servings
November 25, 1967

Light Meals

Turkey Scrapple

3 cups turkey broth or bouillon
½ tsp. onion salt
½ tsp. celery salt
½ tsp. poultry seasoning
1 cup uncooked instant, whole
*   wheat cereal*
2 cups cooked turkey, finely chopped
turkey gravy, as needed

Heat turkey broth or bouillon and onion salt, celery salt, and poultry seasoning. Bring to a rapid boil. Stir in cereal so slow boiling continues. Boil and stir for 10 seconds. Remove from heat. Let stand for five minutes, then stir. Add turkey. Pour into a 1½-quart loaf pan which has been rinsed with cold water. Cover and refrigerate for four to six hours or overnight.

To serve, slice about ¼-inch thick. Brown on both sides on a hot griddle. Serve hot with turkey gravy.
6 to 8 servings
January 16, 1960

There's more than one way to make a scrapple. Here's a delicious alternative to the previous recipe.

Turkey and Stuffing Scrapple

2 chicken bouillon cubes
2 cups hot water
2 cups baked bread stuffing
1 cup gravy
1 tsp. salt
2 cups cooked turkey, chopped
1 cup cornmeal
2 T. fat
gravy, as desired for topping

In a large saucepan, dissolve bouillon cubes in water. Add stuffing, gravy, salt, and turkey; bring mixture to a boil. Add cornmeal gradually and cook for five minutes, stirring constantly. Pour into an oiled 1-quart loaf pan; cool.

Slice into six portions. Melt fat in skillet and fry each portion, turning so that both sides brown evenly. Serve hot with gravy, if used.
6 servings
November 21, 1970

Creamed Turkey on Buttermilk Waffles

4 T. butter
4 T. all-purpose flour
1⅓ cups milk
⅔ cup turkey stock
2 cups cooked turkey, diced
2 T. pimiento, chopped
salt and pepper, to taste

Melt butter in a heavy saucepan. Add flour and mix well. Add milk and stock all at once. Cook, stirring constantly, until thickened. Fold in turkey and pimiento. Heat. Season with salt and pepper.

Serve hot over buttermilk waffles.

Buttermilk Waffles:
2 cups sifted all-purpose flour
2 T. sugar
1½ tsp. baking powder
½ tsp. baking soda
1 tsp. salt
2 eggs, separated
1½ cups buttermilk
½ cup butter, melted

Mix and sift together flour, sugar, baking powder, baking soda, and salt. Beat egg whites until stiff. Add egg yolks to the buttermilk. Beat until blended. Make a well in the dry ingredients. Pour in buttermilk mixture. Stir slightly. Pour in melted butter. Mix just enough to moisten. Fold in egg whites. Bake on hot waffle iron.
4 servings
December 18, 1948

Brunch Pie

1⅔ cups cheese cracker crumbs,
finely rolled (about 40)
¼ cup softened butter or margarine
½ pound ham, cut in strips
½ pound cooked turkey, cut in strips
1 10½-ounce can condensed cream
of chicken soup
¼ cup milk
½ cup Cheddar cheese, grated
3 eggs, beaten
2 tsp. prepared mustard
1 tsp. Worcestershire sauce

Thoroughly blend crumbs and butter or margarine. Press firmly against bottom and sides of a 9-inch pie plate. (The easy way is to press crumbs into place using an 8-inch pie plate.) Layer ham and turkey strips in pie shell, reserving a few strips for garnish. Combine soup, milk, and cheese. Heat, stirring until cheese melts. Add eggs, mustard, and Worcestershire sauce. Pour over meat. Top with reserved strips.

Bake in 300 degree oven 45 minutes, or until knife inserted in center comes out clean.
4 to 6 servings
May 2, 1964

Deluxe Turkey Hash

2 cups frozen hash brown potatoes
¼ cup onion, chopped
2 T. green pepper, chopped
¼ cup butter
2 cups roasted turkey, diced
1 T. pimiento, chopped
¾ tsp. salt
½ tsp. poultry seasoning
⅛ tsp. pepper
½ cup cream or half-and-half

Pan brown potatoes, onion, and green pepper in butter in a heavy skillet. Stir in turkey, pimiento, salt, poultry seasoning, and pepper. Cook over low heat about 10 minutes, stirring frequently. Pour cream over mixture and continue to cook over low heat a few minutes until cream is absorbed.
4 servings
November 26, 1965

Rich Turkey Hash

2 T. onion, chopped
1 T. green pepper, chopped
2 T. butter
1 T. pimiento, chopped
1½ cups roasted turkey, chopped
1½ cups bread cubes, toasted
½ cup cream

Cook onion and green pepper in butter melted in a skillet until tender. Add pimiento and turkey. Stir until mixture is hot. Mix in bread cubes. Pour cream over mixture. Cook over very low heat until cream is absorbed. Serve hot.
4 servings
November 27, 1965

Swedish Turkey

⅓ cup butter
3 T. all-purpose flour
2 tsp. salt
⅛ tsp. pepper
¼ tsp. nutmeg
2 cups milk or half-and-half
2 cups cooked turkey, diced
4 egg yolks, beaten
toast points or pastry shells, as desired
chopped parsley or paprika, as
desired for garnish

Melt butter in saucepan over low heat. Blend in flour, salt, pepper, and nutmeg. Add milk, stirring constantly. Cook and stir until sauce is smooth and thickened. Add turkey and heat through. Add some of the hot sauce to the egg yolks, stirring well. Add egg mixture to turkey mixture. Cook over low heat, stirring gently but continually until mixture thickens.

Serve at once on toast points or in pastry shells. Garnish with paprika or parsley.
6 servings
February 12, 1972

Main Dishes

Gateau of Turkey

Half a pound of cooked turkey, three table-spoonfuls of cooked chopped ham, two teaspoonfuls each of chopped onion and parsley, four tablespoonfuls of bread crumbs, two eggs, half a cupful of stock made from the bones, a few browned bread crumbs, one heaping tablespoonful of drippings and seasoning of salt and pepper.

Butter a pudding basin, sprinkle the crumbs, turning out all that will not stick. Chop the turkey fine, add the ham, bread crumbs, salt, pepper, and parsley. Melt the drippings in a saucepan and fry the onion in it, then add it to the other ingredients. Beat up the eggs and stir them into the mixture. Put it into the prepared basin, taking care not to disturb the coating. Cover the top with a piece of buttered paper and bake in a moderate oven for about three-quarters of an hour. Turn it out onto a hot dish and pour around it some hot tomato or brown sauce.

November 24, 1910

Rotisserie Turkey Hawaiian

1 8- to 10-pound turkey
cooking oil, as needed
1 8¼-ounce can crushed pineapple
1 cup brown sugar
2 T. lemon juice
2 T. prepared mustard
dash of salt

If turkey is frozen, thaw according to directions. Tie wings securely to breast and drumsticks to tail, using twine. Do not stuff turkey. Insert a spit rod and fasten tightly. If desired, insert meat thermometer into thickest part of the breast or thigh. Brush turkey with cooking oil.

Cook for one hour. Meanwhile, prepare basting sauce by mixing pineapple, brown sugar, lemon juice, mustard, and salt. Continue cooking turkey, basting every 30 minutes with sauce. Total cooking time will be 3½ to 4 hours.

Before carving, let the turkey sit for at least 10 minutes.

Serve either hot or cold. Good with Savory Lemon Rice, and your favorite salad. 10 to 15 servings

Savory Lemon Rice

1¾ cloves garlic, minced
2 T. butter
1½ cups chicken broth
1¾ tsp. salt
1½ cups long-grain rice
1½ T. parsley
2 tsp. lemon juice

Saute garlic in butter in a medium sized saucepan. Add broth and salt and bring to a boil. Stir in rice. Cook according to package directions. Fluff with a fork, add parsley and lemon juice.
4 to 6 servings
July 2, 1977

Roasted Turkey on a Spit

1 8- to 10-pound ready-to-cook turkey
3 cups wild rice, cooked
¼ cup parsley, minced
½ cup mushrooms, sliced
2 T. onion, grated
½ cup butter, melted
½ tsp. salt
⅛ tsp. poultry seasoning
cooking oil, as needed

Rinse and dry turkey; sprinkle body cavity with salt. Combine remaining ingredients. Fill body cavity; tie or pin to secure opening. Pin neck skin to back; tie bird together and balance on spit. Brush bird with oil at frequent intervals; roast four to five hours or until done.
12 or more servings
August 15, 1964

Cooking on the grill is a great way to prepare turkey. Simply baste the bird with one of the following sauces as it cooks.

Turkey Barbecue Sauces

To prepare any of these sauces, combine all ingredients. Mix well.

New England Style
½ cup vegetable oil
½ cup lemon juice
½ tsp. poultry seasoning
¼ tsp. garlic salt
¼ tsp. coarse black pepper
¼ tsp. paprika
½ tsp. monosodium glutamate

Southern Style
6 ounces tomato puree
¼ cup lemon juice
2 T. prepared mustard
4 T. brown sugar
1 tsp. instant onion, minced
½ tsp. garlic salt
½ tsp. monosodium glutamate
½ tsp. salt

Western Style
Ingredients for Southern Style Sauce plus 2 cubes beef bouillon dissolved in ½ cup water or concentrated beef stock

Barbecue Sauce Glazes
Dissolve one and one-half tablespoons of cornstarch in two tablespoons of water and add to each cup of barbecue sauce. Cook until the mixture clears and thickens. Spread over turkey while hot when you remove it from the grill.
November 14, 1970

Honey Lemon Glaze for Turkey

⅔ cup honey
¼ cup lemon juice
½ cup water
1½ T. cornstarch

Combine honey and lemon juice in saucepan and bring to a boil. Add water to cornstarch to make a smooth paste. Gradually add to honey, stirring constantly. Cook until glaze thickens and becomes clear. Spoon over roasted turkey to glaze the surface.
April 1, 1972

Italian Turkey Bake

4 ounces egg noodles, uncooked
⅓ cup butter, melted
6 T. all-purpose flour
2 cups chicken broth
¾ cup milk
3 T. sauterne or sherry
½ tsp. salt
dash pepper
⅓ cup Parmesan cheese, grated
6 slices cooked turkey
2 cans whole tomatoes (1 pound
   each), drained and sliced
2 tsp. sweet basil flakes
1 T. parsley, chopped

Preheat oven to 375 degrees.
Cook noodles until tender in boiling water. Meanwhile, blend butter and flour in saucepan. Gradually add broth and milk; cook until sauce thickens, stirring constantly. Simmer 2 minutes, then remove from heat. Add sauterne or sherry, salt, pepper, and cheese.
In a 2-quart casserole, form layers using half the drained noodles, 3 slices turkey, and half the tomatoes. Sprinkle with half the basil. Top with half the sauce. Repeat layers. Sprinkle casserole with parsley.
Bake in oven for 15 to 20 minutes.
6 servings
January 25, 1975

When you want a treat that will appeal to teenagers who are tired of hamburgers and pizza, try a Mexican theme. Set your table with a Mexican motif and serve Mexican goodies next time you have the teens over.

In Mexico the tortilla is the staff of life. Tortillas, thin corn or wheat pancake-like breads, are readily available at your supermarket—fresh, canned, or frozen. The canned enchilada sauce used in this recipe is found in the foreign food section, and may be purchased either mild or hot. Remember, "hot" may bring a few tears to your eyes!

Enchiladas are simple meat pies made of tortillas wrapped around a meat and vegetable filling and cooked in a peppery sauce. The teens, and adults too, will like these.

Turkey Enchiladas

½ cup onion, chopped
¼ cup butter
2 cups cooked turkey, chopped
1 17-ounce can golden cream-style corn
1 16-ounce can whole tomatoes, undrained
¼ cup cornmeal
3 tsp. chili powder
1 tsp. salt
¼ tsp. garlic powder
18 corn tortillas
hot oil, as needed
1 cup sharp Cheddar cheese, shredded

Sauce:
1 10-ounce can enchilada sauce
1½ cups sour cream

In a large skillet saute onion in butter until transparent. Stir in turkey, corn, tomatoes, cornmeal, chili powder, salt, and garlic powder. Simmer, uncovered, for 15 minutes.

Dip tortillas in hot oil to soften. Spread about ¼ cup filling on each tortilla, roll up, and place seam side down in a shallow baking dish.

Make sauce by combining enchilada sauce and sour cream; stir until smooth. Pour over tortillas. Sprinkle with cheese.

Bake in 350 degree oven for 20 to 30 minutes.
8 to 10 servings
March 27, 1977

Another South-of-the-Border inspired dish.

Fiesta Turkey Casserole

¼ cup butter
3 cups cooked turkey, diced
1 cup onion, chopped
1 1¼-ounce package chili seasoning
  mix
1 8-ounce can tomato sauce
⅔ cup water
1 5-ounce can whole mushrooms,
  drained
1 pound cooked kidney beans
2 small (2¼-ounce) packages corn
  chips
½ cup sliced, pitted black olives
1 cup sharp Cheddar cheese, shredded

Melt butter in saucepan. Add turkey and brown slightly, stirring occasionally. Add onion, seasoning mix, tomato sauce, and water. Mix well. Bring mixture to boil; cover and simmer 15 minutes, stirring frequently to prevent sticking. Alternate layers of turkey mixture with mushrooms, beans, corn chips, olives, and cheese in a 2-quart casserole, ending with cheese and corn chips.

Bake in 350 degree oven for 30 minutes.
6 servings
March 27, 1977

Turkey Croquettes

One and one-half cups chopped, cold turkey; one-fourth teaspoon celery salt, one-half teaspoon salt, pepper, a few drops onion juice, and one cup thick, white sauce. Mix these ingredients in the order mentioned, cool and shape as desired; roll in beaten egg; cover with fine crumbs and cook in deep fat.
December 4, 1913

Party Turkey 'n' Cream

¼ cup onion, minced
2 T. butter or margarine
2 T. all-purpose flour
¼ cup milk
2 T. sherry (optional)
1 cup sour cream
2 tomatoes, peeled and finely
  chopped
1 bay leaf
¼ tsp. salt
¼ tsp. sugar
12 slices roasted turkey (about 12
  ounces)

Saute onion in butter or margarine until tender. Stir in flour and cook until golden brown. Add milk, sherry, and sour cream. Blend until smooth. Add tomatoes, bay leaf, salt, and sugar. Stir. Cover and simmer 20 minutes. Place turkey slices in sauce. Cover and continue cooking 5 to 10 minutes, just long enough to heat turkey through. Remove bay leaf.

Serve over Confetti Rice.
4 servings

Confetti Rice

1 cup uncooked rice
2 cups chicken broth
1 T. butter or margarine
2 T. parsley, chopped
2 T. pimientos, diced

Cook rice in broth until tender. Add butter, parsley, and pimiento just before serving.
4 servings
November 15, 1975

Turkey and Sausage Casserole

2 T. butter
2 cups cooked turkey, chopped
1 cup cooked sausage, chopped
2 T. parsley, chopped
2 T. chives, chopped
1 cup bite-size cereal, crushed to ½ cup
½ tsp. lemon rind, grated
½ cup cream of mushroom soup
chopped parsley, as needed for garnish

Melt butter; slightly brown turkey and sausage. Add parsley, chives, cereal, lemon rind, and soup. Mix thoroughly. Cover and cook 25 to 30 minutes over low heat.

To serve, sprinkle additional parsley over top.
4 servings
January 4, 1966

Hot 'n' Spicy Turkey

⅓ cup green onion, sliced
2 T. butter or margarine
1 cup celery, sliced
½ cup green pepper, diced
3 cups cooked rice
1 cup sour cream
½ tsp. salt
¼ tsp. cayenne pepper
1 cup Cheddar cheese, shredded
20-ounce can pineapple tidbits, drained
2 cups cooked turkey, diced

Saute onions in butter. Remove from heat and add celery and green pepper. Combine rice with sour cream, salt, pepper, and one-half cup of the cheese. Layer in an oiled 2-quart casserole one-third of the rice mixture, half the pineapple, half the celery mixture, and half the turkey. Repeat the layers. Cover with remaining rice and top with the remaining cheese.

Bake in a 350 degree oven for 35 to 45 minutes, until heated through and bubbly.

Complete the meal with a tossed green salad and rye or whole wheat bread.
6 servings
November 15, 1975

Turkey Chow Mein

2 to 3 cups cooked turkey, cut in strips
2 T. butter or margarine
3 T. onion, chopped
1 tsp. salt
2 chicken bouillon cubes
1½ cups boiling water
2 T. green pepper, chopped
2 cups celery, diagonally-sliced
1 can bean sprouts, drained
3 T. cornstarch
1 T. (or more) soy sauce
6 T. cold water
Chinese noodles or hot rice, as needed

Brown turkey in butter or margarine along with onion. Add salt. Dissolve bouillon cubes in hot water; stir into meat, cover, and simmer for 10 minutes. Add green pepper and celery; cover and cook slowly 5 to 10 minutes, or until celery is tender. Stir in bean sprouts and heat. Blend cornstarch and soy sauce in cold water until smooth. Add to meat and cook until thick.

Serve on Chinese noodles or rice.
4 to 6 servings
November 21, 1964

News about the war filled even the food pages of magazines during 1943. Meals that saved meat, sugar, flour, and — of course — money, were constant reminders of the war effort. But turkey was available and welcome.

"Turkey — our traditional Thanksgiving bird — can again reign at holiday dinners. Less than 10 percent of our turkeys enlisted for the soldiers', sailors' and marines' holiday dinners, leaving 445 million pounds of turkey hens and gobblers to grace civilian tables."
Wallaces Farmer And Iowa Homestead, November 20, 1943

Turkey Budget Pie

1½ cups cooked turkey, chopped
1½ cups cooked potatoes, diced
½ cup cooked carrots or celery, diced
2 T. onion, finely minced
1½ cups medium white sauce or
    canned cream soup
salt and pepper, to taste
½ cup cheese, grated
pastry to cover top of baking dish

Preheat oven to 400 degrees.

Combine turkey, potatoes, carrots or celery, and onion. Add cream sauce, salt and pepper, and cheese. Place in shallow baking dish.

Cover turkey mixture with pastry, pressing firmly just below edge of dish to seal. Cut pastry turkey from scraps and arrange on top. Cut slits in pastry.

Bake until pastry is nicely browned and filling begins to bubble. Serve hot from baking dish.
4 or 5 servings
November 20, 1943

Turkey Tetrazzini

2 T. butter
½ cup onion, chopped
1 3-ounce can sliced mushrooms
5 T. all-purpose flour
1 tsp. garlic salt
½ tsp. salt
½ tsp. sage
½ tsp. oregano
⅛ tsp. pepper
2½ cups milk
2 cups cooked turkey, chopped
½ cup cooked carrots, thinly sliced
¼ pound spaghetti, cut into 2-inch
    pieces and cooked
grated cheese, as needed for garnish
    (optional)

Melt butter in a large skillet; add onion and mushrooms. Saute until onion is tender. Blend in flour. Stir in garlic salt, salt, sage, oregano, pepper, milk, turkey, and carrots.

Cook over medium heat until mixture thickens slightly, stirring occasionally. Place spaghetti in bottom of a 2-quart casserole; pour turkey mixture over top.

Bake in 350 degree oven for 20 minutes, or until sauce bubbles.

To serve, garnish with cheese, if desired.
4 servings
December 19, 1959

An old "tried and true" recipe from the 1930s.

Turkey Almond and Celery Scallop

2 cups bread cubes
¼ cup almonds
1 T. butter
1 cup celery, sliced
1 cup water
¼ tsp. salt
1 cup cooked turkey, diced
½ cup turkey stock
milk, as needed
3 T. butter
3 T. all-purpose flour
½ tsp. salt

Toast bread cubes to a golden brown in a moderate oven. Slice almonds lengthwise into thin slivers and toast to a light golden brown in one tablespoon butter in moderate oven. Cook celery in one cup water and one-quarter teaspoon salt. When tender, drain off water into a measuring cup. Add turkey stock and enough milk to make one and one-half cups. (If no stock is available, use one-half cup more milk.) Make a white sauce of this liquid with the three tablespoons butter, flour, and one-half teaspoon salt. Combine almonds and turkey. Place about one-third of the bread cubes in bottom of the casserole, cover with one-half of the turkey, then one-half of the celery. Make another layer of bread cubes, then turkey, then celery. Pour white sauce over and cover with remaining bread cubes.

Bake in 350 degree oven for 20 to 25 minutes.
4 servings
December 3, 1938

83

Western Turkey Casserole

⅓ cup butter
¼ cup all-purpose flour
1½ tsp. salt
⅛ tsp. pepper
1½ tsp. curry powder
½ tsp. powdered ginger
3 cups milk
1 T. soy sauce
1 pound canned, drained Chinese
    vegetables or 1 pound package of
    frozen Chinese vegetables, thawed
10 ounces cooked turkey, cubed
2 cups cooked rice
3 ounces Chow Mein noodles

Preheat oven to 375 degrees.

Melt butter in saucepan. Blend in flour, salt, pepper, curry powder, and ginger. Add milk and soy sauce; cook, stirring constantly, until sauce is thickened and smooth. Fold in vegetables and turkey.

Place an equal amount of rice in six 10-ounce individual casseroles; top each with an equal amount of turkey mixture and noodles.

Bake in oven until hot and bubbly, about 15 minutes.

6 servings
February 12, 1972

Turkey Triumph

1 cup celery, sliced
1 green pepper, cut into squares
2 chicken bouillon cubes, dissolved
    in 2 cups boiling water
2 T. cornstarch blended with ½ cup
    cold water
4 cups roast turkey, cut up
1 tsp. ground ginger
1 tsp. salt
hot cooked rice or noodle nests, as
    desired
½ cup almonds, roasted and slivered

Drop celery and green pepper into boiling, salted water for two minutes. Drain. Blend bouillon and cornstarch mixtures in a skillet. Cook, stirring, until thickened. Add turkey, celery, green pepper, ginger, and salt. Cover and cook for 15 minutes.

Serve over hot cooked rice or noodle nests. Sprinkle almonds on top.

4 servings
November 21, 1970

Turkey-Green Bean Parmesan

2 pkgs. frozen French-style green
    beans
3 T. butter
3 T. all-purpose flour
¼ tsp. salt
dash pepper
½ tsp. prepared mustard
1½ cups milk
⅓ cup mayonnaise
grated peel and juice of 1 lemon
1½ to 2 cups cooked turkey, cubed
½ cup Parmesan cheese, grated

Cook beans as directed on package; drain. Melt butter in saucepan. Blend in flour, salt, pepper, and mustard. Add milk and continue stirring constantly until thickened. Remove from heat. Fold in mayonnaise and lemon peel and juice. Stir in turkey.

Spread green beans in bottom of a buttered baking dish. Pour in turkey mixture. Top with Parmesan cheese.

Bake in 350 degree oven 30 to 40 minutes.

6 servings
February 11, 1979

Turkey in the stuffing instead of the other way around. Here is a delicious casserole for the day after Thanksgiving.

Topsy Turvy Turkey

4½ cups bread crumbs
¼ cup celery, diced
¼ cup parsley, minced
⅛ tsp. thyme
⅛ tsp. pepper
⅓ cup water
¼ cup butter
2 cups cooked turkey, cubed
2 cups cooked vegetables, diced
1 can condensed cream of celery soup

Preheat oven to 400 degrees.

Combine bread crumbs, celery, parsley, thyme, and pepper. Heat water with butter and pour over crumb mixture. Toss lightly. Pat half the crumb mixture onto sides and bottom of an oiled 2-quart casserole. Mix turkey with vegetables and soup and spoon into the casserole. Top with remaining crumb mixture.

Bake in oven for 35 minutes. Remove from oven, let stand five minutes, and then invert onto a serving dish.
6 servings
November 16, 1957

Baked Turkey Tempter

4 ounces elbow macaroni or spaghetti
2 tsp. salt
3 cups boiling water
4 T. butter
¼ cup all-purpose flour
3 T. nonfat dry milk solids
½ tsp. salt
⅛ tsp. pepper
1 cup water
1 10½-ounce can condensed cream
   of mushroom soup
¾ cup cooked peas
1 cup cooked turkey (or chicken),
   chopped
½ cup American cheese (2 ounces),
   shredded

Add macaroni or spaghetti to 3 cups rapidly boiling, salted water. Boil, stirring constantly, for 2 minutes. Cover, remove from heat, and let stand 10 minutes. Melt butter in saucepan. Stir in flour, milk solids, salt, and pepper. Add 1 cup water gradually, stirring constantly, and then blend in soup. Cook mixture until thickened, stirring constantly. Rinse macaroni or spaghetti with warm water and drain well; add to sauce along with turkey and peas. Turn into oiled 1½-quart casserole. Sprinkle cheese over top.

Bake in 350 degree oven for about 20 minutes.
4 servings
November 16, 1957

Make-ahead meals are a real convenience when the cook works outside of the home all day. This recipe makes approximately 20 one-cup portions, and freezes very well in pint and quart freezer containers.

Turkey-Macaroni Casserole

1¼ quarts shell or other macaroni
2 quarts boiling salted water
⅔ cup butter or margarine, melted
1¼ cups sifted all-purpose flour
2 quarts hot milk
1½ T. salt
¼ tsp. pepper
1 tsp. marjoram
2½ cups cheese, grated
¾ cup pimiento, chopped
1¼ quarts cooked turkey, diced
grated cheese, as needed for topping

Cook macaroni in boiling salted water for 15 minutes or until almost tender; drain and rinse with water. Combine butter with flour, stir in milk, and cook until thick. Add salt, pepper, marjoram, cheese, pimiento, and turkey.

To serve immediately, place in oiled casserole(s) and top with grated cheese. Bake uncovered in 350 degree oven for 30 to 40 minutes.

To freeze, cool casserole mixture quickly, pack in freezer containers, leaving head space, seal, and freeze. To prepare for serving, add a topping of grated cheese and bake uncovered at 400 degrees until food is heated through, about 45 minutes for pints, or one hour for quarts.
20 servings, about 1 cup each
July 15, 1967

Turkey Mornay with Noodles

6 ounces noodles, cooked and drained
¼ cup butter
¼ cup all-purpose flour
½ tsp. salt
2 cups milk
½ pound Cheddar cheese, shredded
¼ pound mushrooms, sliced and
    sauteed in butter, or 1 4-ounce
    can mushrooms
2 pimientos, diced
2 cups cooked turkey (or chicken),
    diced
crushed corn flakes or potato chips,
    as needed for topping

Cook noodles in turkey or chicken stock until tender. Drain. Melt butter in a 3-quart saucepan; blend in flour; add salt and gradually add milk, stirring constantly. Heat until thickened and smooth. Stir in cheese, mushrooms, and pimiento. When cheese melts, stir in turkey and noodles. Pour into a buttered 2½-quart casserole. Sprinkle top with corn flakes or chips.

Bake in 325 degree oven for about 40 minutes.
6 to 8 servings
November 15, 1958

86

Turkey Almond

1 cup celery, cut in 1-inch pieces
1 onion, sliced
2 T. butter
2 cups cooked turkey, diced
½ cup mushrooms, sauteed in butter,
    or ½ cup canned mushrooms
1 T. cornstarch
3 T. soy sauce
1 cup chicken broth or consomme
½ to 1 cup toasted almonds
hot cooked rice, as needed

Saute celery and onion in butter. Add turkey and mushrooms. Heat. Combine cornstarch, soy sauce, and broth. Stir slowly into turkey mixture. Bring to boil, and allow to boil for one minute. Stir in almonds.
    Serve hot on rice.
6 servings
January 16, 1958

Turkey Swirls with Cranberry Sauce

2 cups whole cranberry sauce
1½ cups sifted all-purpose flour
2 tsp. baking powder
1 tsp. salt
¼ cup shortening
½ to ⅔ cup milk
1 cup cooked turkey, finely chopped
cranberry sauce, for topping, if desired

Preheat oven to 450 degrees.
    Spoon cranberry sauce into 8-inch square pan; spread evenly over bottom. Sift together flour, baking powder, and salt. Cut or rub in shortening until mixture is crumbly. Add milk to make soft dough. Turn onto lightly floured board or pastry cloth and knead gently 30 seconds. Roll out to 9-inch square and spread turkey evenly over top. Roll up like a jelly roll. Seal edge securely. Cut into 1-inch slices. Arrange, cut side down, on top of cranberry sauce.
    Bake in oven for 30 to 35 minutes, or until golden brown. Serve hot with additional cranberry sauce, if desired.
4 to 6 servings
January 9, 1965

Ham and Turkey Ring

2 cups cooked ham, ground
2 cups cooked turkey, ground
½ cup nut meats, chopped
¾ cup nonfat dry milk
2 eggs
½ tsp. powdered thyme
½ tsp. poultry seasoning
1 tsp. salt
2 cups whole cranberry sauce

Combine ham, turkey, nut meats, nonfat dry milk, eggs, thyme, poultry seasoning, and salt. Mix well. Spoon cranberry sauce into oiled 1-quart ring mold. Press meat mixture firmly into mold.
    Bake in 350 degree oven about 30 minutes, or until lightly browned on top. Unmold to serve.
6 servings
November 27, 1965

Curried Turkey Ring

6 ounces medium noodles
1 T. salt
4½ cups water, boiling
1½ cups milk
1 cup (4 ounces) cheddar cheese,
    shredded
2 eggs
½ tsp. salt
½ tsp. curry powder
⅛ tsp. pepper
½ cup soft bread crumbs
¼ cup raisins

Filling:
2 to 3 cups roasted turkey, chopped
leftover gravy, as desired for topping

Add noodles and salt to water; boil rapidly, stirring constantly for two minutes. Cover, remove from heat and let stand for 10 minutes. Scald milk, add cheese, and stir over low heat until cheese is melted and mixture is smooth. Beat eggs in large mixing bowl; beat in salt, curry powder, and pepper. Add milk/cheese mixture gradually, stirring constantly. Rinse noodles with warm water; drain well. Add crumbs, raisins, and noodles to milk mixture. Mix well.

Spoon into well oiled 8-inch mold; set mold in larger pan which has one inch of hot water in it. Bake in 350 degree oven until set, about 45 minutes. Remove from oven and let cool 10 minutes. Loosen noodle ring from sides of mold with knife or spatula.

To serve, unmold on platter and fill center with leftover turkey and gravy.
6 servings
February 3, 1962

Turkey Spanish Rice

2 slices bacon
1 onion, chopped
½ green pepper, chopped
½ cup uncooked rice
1 1-pound can stewed tomatoes
1½ cups canned tomato juice
½ tsp. paprika
1 tsp. salt
¼ tsp. pepper
2 cups cooked turkey, cubed

Cook bacon until crisp; remove from pan and drain. When cool, crumble bacon. Cook onion and pepper in bacon fat until tender. Add rice, bacon, tomatoes, tomato juice, paprika, salt, pepper, and turkey. Bring to a boil. Pour into an oiled casserole.

Bake, covered, in a 350 degree oven for about one hour, or until rice is tender.
6 to 8 servings
November 13, 1971

American-Style Turkey Fried Rice

1 cup cooked turkey, diced
1 T. soy sauce
¼ cup oil
1 cup uncooked rice
2 cups chicken bouillon
2 T. onion, chopped
¼ cup celery, sliced
¼ cup green pepper, minced
1 egg, slightly beaten
½ cup Chinese cabbage or head
    lettuce, finely shredded

Combine turkey and soy sauce. Let stand while cooking rice. Heat oil in large skillet and add rice. Fry, stirring frequently, until rice is golden brown. Add bouillon and turkey. Cover and simmer until rice is almost tender and liquid is absorbed. Add onion, celery, and green pepper and cook, uncovered, a few minutes. Push rice to sides of skillet and add egg. Stir slightly and cook until almost set, then combine with rice mixture. Stir in cabbage or lettuce.

Serve immediately.
4 servings
November 15, 1975

The mushroom sauce that follows the next two recipes is delicious on both.

Turkey Cheese Turnovers

Cheese Pastry:
2¼ cups all-purpose flour
⅔ cup shortening
1 cup cheese, grated
4 T. ice water, or as needed

Cut shortening and cheese in flour. Sprinkle the dough with water, and lightly mix until you can gather the dough into a ball. Roll out pastry on a floured board to ⅛-inch thickness and cut in 6-inch squares or 4-inch circles. Chill while you make filling.

Filling:
4 T. butter
2 T. onion, minced
½ cup celery, finely diced
3 T. all-purpose flour
1 tsp. salt
⅛ tsp. pepper
1 cup milk
2 cups cooked turkey, diced
2 T. parsley, minced

Preheat oven to 450 degrees.

Melt butter; add onion and celery and cook over low heat until tender. Blend in flour, salt, and pepper. Gradually stir in milk and cook until mixture boils and thickens, stirring constantly. Add turkey and parsley; remove from heat.

To assemble, mound filling on each piece of pastry; fold pastry to make triangles or half-circles and press edges together with a fork. Prick tops to let steam escape.

Bake in 450 degree oven for 10 minutes; reduce heat to 400 degrees and bake 15 minutes longer, until lightly browned.

Serve with mushroom sauce.

4 to 6 servings
December 19, 1959

Curried Turkey Casserole

2 T. butter
½ cup onions, sliced
1 #2 can pineapple tidbits (approximately 20-ounce can)
1¼ cups turkey or chicken broth or bouillon
2 T. cornstarch
1½ tsp. salt
1 tsp. curry powder
½ cup green pepper, chopped
3 cups ½-inch toasted bread crumbs
1½ cups cooked turkey (or chicken), chopped
¼ cup almonds, slivered

Melt butter in skillet; add onions and simmer until transparent. Drain pineapple, reserving liquid. Add broth to pineapple liquid to make 2 cups. Dissolve cornstarch, salt, and curry powder in liquid. Add liquid and green pepper to onions in skillet. Cook until sauce thickens, stirring constantly.

Arrange layers of half of the bread crumbs, turkey, pineapple, and almonds in an oiled 1½-quart casserole and cover with half the sauce. Repeat layers, ending with bread cubes, and pour other half of the sauce over the top.

Bake in 350 degree oven for 30 minutes.

Serve with Mushroom Sauce
December 19, 1959

Mushroom Sauce

½ pound mushrooms, sliced
1 T. onion, minced
4 T. butter
4 T. all-purpose flour
1 tsp. salt
⅛ tsp. pepper
¼ tsp. paprika
1 tsp. Worcestershire sauce
2 cups milk

Saute mushrooms and onion in butter until tender. Blend in flour, salt, pepper, paprika, and Worcestershire. Stir in milk and cook over low heat until mixture boils and thickens, stirring constantly.
4 servings
December 19, 1959

4
Why You Probably Won't Eat Duck

If the National Duckling Council has its way, February 20 would be an important day in your life. It certainly is important to them.

Why? February 20 is the day of Chinese New Year, and it is traditionally celebrated with roast duck. If the Duckling Council could get us to eat duck on Chinese New Year the way we eat turkeys on Thanksgiving, it would be duck soup for the nation's duck growers.

Actually, and to be technical about it, it's not duck that they're trying to get you to eat. The fact is, you'd have a hard time buying duck because almost all the duck retailed in this country is actually duckling—a bird weighing around four and a half to five pounds and not more than 55 days old.

The variety you're most likely to see in the frozen food section of your supermarket is often labelled "Long Island Duckling." It's actually a White Pekin, the same variety you can find in some Chinese groceries.

Incidentally, "Pekin" is the correct name for the bird. If you're in a Chinese restaurant ordering "Peking Duck," you're choosing a particular method of preparation—not the kind of bird.

There is also another major commercial duck that you may come across—the Muscovy Duck. It's unusual among ducks because it roosts like a chicken, has a breast like a modern turkey, and has a flavor that some connoisseurs compare to veal. The Muscovy is exceptionally juicy with intense flavor.

Today's breeders are constantly working to select and breed ducks for more meat, better cooking qualities, greater disease resistance, and better feed conversions ratios. To help you get the most for your money when buying and serving their modern product, here are some of their tips.

When buying fresh birds—as opposed to frozen—make sure that the skin is unblemished and smooth with no discoloration. The breast should be noticeably plump and meaty.

A frozen bird has the same tell-tale signs of quality, or lack of it, as an unfrozen one. Unfortunately, the bird will usually be wrapped in opaque plastic and you won't be able to see these signs. Nevertheless, there are several key things you can check, and once you know about them, you'll be able to select a better bird.

First, make sure that the wrapping is entirely intact, with no holes or rips. Even a tiny tear can mean freezer burn and the adjacent meat will be dried out, tough, and tasteless.

Second, make sure there is no pinkish ice around the meat. Birds are dried before freezing, so if you find ice crystals, it means that somewhere in the packing or shipping or storage, the bird has been allowed to partially thaw and has been refrozen. If this has happened, you know that the bird will have lost much of its special quality and flavor. Look for another bird.

When it comes to cooking duckling, growers recommend that any stuffing be cooked separately since the rendered fat can soak into the stuffing. In fact, if you've never cooked duckling before, you'll be surprised at just how much fat will end up in your roasting pan.

The high fat content of the Pekin Duckling, coupled with its relatively heavy frame, means you should allow at least one and a half pounds per serving. The Muscovy Duck has a somewhat more favorable percentage of edible meat per pound, so with a Muscovy, you can safely allow between a pound and a pound and a quarter per serving.

Whichever duckling or even duck that you choose, why not try one for Chinese New Year? Or better yet, try them any time of the year and celebrate with duck!

Menu for Roast Duck Dinner
Serves 8

*Ducklings, Crisp-Roasted
with Foil**
Spiced Apple Garnish*
Rice Like Wild*
Crisp Green Salad
Brussels Sprouts
Grandma's Lemon Cream Pie*
Coffee or Tea

*Recipes included

Ducklings, Crisp-Roasted with Foil

2 4- to 5-pound ducklings
2 cloves garlic
2 tsp. salt
2 T. curry powder
½ tsp. pepper

Sauce:
1½ cups cider
½ tsp. salt
¼ cup brown sugar

Rinse and dry ducklings. Crush garlic in salt. Add curry powder and pepper. Rub ducks inside and out with this mixture. Tie feet. Bind wings close to body with string.

Line two shallow roasting pans with heavy duty aluminum foil using a broiler pan from your range and a roasting pan. Place a rack in one pan and add ducklings. Roast one hour in 350 degree oven. When most of fat has drained from ducks after first hour of roasting, quickly transfer them to the clean foil-lined pan by lifting rack and ducks together. The foil and fat in first lined pan are then disposed of and pan left clean.

Brush with sauce made by simmering cider, salt, and brown sugar until thickened slightly. Continue roasting one hour to one and a quarter hours longer, brushing with sauce occasionally. Ducks are done when leg joints move easily. Transfer to carving board. Cut each duckling into four quarters, using poultry shears and a sharp knife.

Choose vegetables such as colorful red cabbage cooked with piquant flavorings, brussels sprouts, and baked acorn squash to complement the rich flavor of duck.
8 servings
October 16, 1959

Spiced Apple Garnish

1 cup water
½ cup granulated sugar
½ cup brown sugar, packed
½ tsp. ground cloves
½ tsp. cinnamon
3 red apples
raisins, as needed

Combine water, sugars, cinnamon, and cloves in small saucepan; heat for 10 minutes. Cut apples in half; remove cores. Place in baking dish, cut side up; fill centers with raisins. Pour sauce over apples.

Bake in 325 degree oven for 45 minutes to one hour, or until apples are soft. Baste two or three times during baking. Serve as garnish with roast bird.
November 25, 1967

Rice Like Wild

2 cups uncooked rice, rinsed
2 beef bouillon cubes
2 cans beef broth
½ cup butter
2 cans mushrooms with juice
water, as needed
6 T. onion, minced
1 tsp. pepper
2 tsp. marjoram

In a two-quart casserole, mix rice, bouillon, broth, butter, mushrooms, onion, pepper, and marjoram. Add water to juice from mushrooms to make two cups.

Bake in a 350 degree oven for one hour.
6 to 8 servings

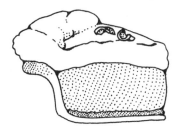

Grandma's Lemon Cream Pie

Pie Filling:

1 cup sugar
5 T. cornstarch
¼ tsp. salt
2 cups milk
3 egg yolks
3 T. butter
1 tsp. lemon peel, grated
⅓ cup lemon juice
1 9-inch pie shell, baked

Meringue:

¼ tsp. salt
1 tsp. lemon juice
¼ tsp. vanilla
3 egg whites
6 T. sugar

To prepare filling, mix sugar, cornstarch, and salt in a saucepan. Add milk gradually and stir until smooth. Cook over low heat, stirring constantly, until smooth and thickened throughout, about 10 minutes. Stir a small amount of hot mixture into egg yolks. Gradually combine yolks with remaining hot mixture. Continue cooking, stirring constantly, about five minutes. Remove from heat. Add butter, lemon peel and juice; blend thoroughly. Set aside while preparing the meringue.

To prepare meringue, add salt, lemon juice, and vanilla to egg whites in mixing bowl; beat until foamy. Add sugar one tablespoon at a time, beating constantly. Beat until sugar is dissolved and whites are glossy and stand in soft peaks. Pour hot filling into baked pie shell. Spread meringue on filling, starting with small amounts at the edges and fixing it to the crust at every point. Allow no space between meringue and crust. Cover pie with remaining meringue, spreading evenly in swirls.

Bake in a 350 degree-oven for 12 to 15 minutes or until tops of irregular surface are lightly browned. Cool at room temperature.
One 9-inch pie
September 4, 1971

Roast Reichardt Duckling

1 4- to 5-pound duckling
salt, to taste
approximately ½ cup honey

Preheat oven to 400 degrees.

Wash duckling and drain it. Season the cavity with salt, and then place the duckling on a rack in a roasting pan, breast side up.

Roast, uncovered, in oven, allowing 25 minutes per pound. At the halfway point, pierce all over with a fork to permit the melted fat to drain off. Turn the bird over and brush with honey. After 15-20 minutes turn the duckling again so breast is up and brush with more honey. Continue roasting another 15 minutes. Skin will be nicely browned and crisp.

To serve, cut the bird in quarters.
4 servings
December 21, 1984

Bread Sauce for Game

Sift a pint of bread crumbs, put two-thirds of a pint of milk in a saucepan, add a little grated onion, set on the stove, season with cayenne pepper, salt and a little nutmeg, let come to a boil; add half the bread crumbs. Fry the remainder in butter until brown.
December 6, 1900

Stewed Duck

Clean and divide the duck as for fricassee. Put it into a saucepan with several slices of ham or salt pork minced fine. Cover closely and let stew slowly for an hour. Then stir in a large onion chopped fine, half a teaspoon of powdered sage, same of parsley, one tablespoon catsup, salt and pepper to taste. Stew until thoroughly tender, then add some browned flour mixed to a paste with water and a pinch of sugar. Boil up once and serve.
January 16, 1903

Mock Duck

Cut two tenderloins through lengthwise. Open and pound flat. Chop two apples, add salt and pepper to taste and cover one tenderloin with the mixture. Then cover again with a mixture of boiled prunes from which the pits have been removed. Place the second tenderloin over this and roll and tie securely. Brown in two tablespoons of butter. Put it in a baking dish and cover with a cup of sweet or sour cream.
June 23, 1927

If you're a hunter or have friends who are, you may be able to find duck, not duckling. Here's a quick-to-cook recipe from the 1970s, followed by a longer version from 1947.

Quick-Roasted Wild Duck

½ orange for each duck used
wild duck(s)
melted butter, as needed
red or white wine or orange juice,
*   as desired*
salt and pepper, to taste

Preheat oven to 450 to 475 degrees.

Place one orange half inside the cavity of each duck. Place ducks on a rack in a shallow pan.

Roast in oven, basting well with melted butter and wine or with melted butter and orange juice. Roast for 20 to 30 minutes. Season with salt and pepper.
October 26, 1974

Wild Duck

wild duck(s)
strongly salted water, as needed
salt and pepper, to taste
apples, celery, and onion, as needed
bacon or fat pork, as needed

Soak ducks, after they are dressed, in pan of salt water for two or three hours. Dry thoroughly. Rub the inside and outside with salt and pepper. Stuff with apples, celery, and onion. Cover the breast and back with strips of bacon or fat pork. Place ducks, breast side down, in large uncovered roasting pan.

Roast in 300 degree oven. When ducks begin to turn brown, cover roaster and cook ducks very slowly. Baste every 20 minutes and continue to roast for three hours. During last half hour, remove cover and turn ducks on back so breast may brown.
November 1, 1947

Oven Barbecued Duck

2 ducks, cleaned and halved
1 clove garlic, crushed
¼ cup butter, melted
¼ cup salad oil
¼ cup lemon juice
1 T. onion, grated
1 T. paprika
⅓ cup catsup
⅛ tsp. pepper

Preheat oven to 400 degrees.

Place duck halves, split side down, in a shallow baking pan. Rub with garlic and brush with butter.

Roast, uncovered, for 10 to 15 minutes. Meanwhile, combine the remaining ingredients and heat them to simmering. Reduce oven temperature to 350 degrees and baste with the sauce every 10 minutes until ducks are tender, about 40 to 50 minutes.
6 servings
October 22, 1977

Baked Wild Duck in Brown-In Bag

1 T. all-purpose flour
1 cup orange juice
1 duck
melted butter, as needed
salt, to taste
chopped apple and celery, as needed

Shake one tablespoon flour in a small (10 × 16-inch) Brown-In Bag, and place in a two-inch deep roasting pan. Pour orange juice into bag, and stir until flour is well mixed. Brush duck with butter. Salt cavity and outside. Fill cavity with apple and celery. Place duck in bag. Close bag with twist tie, and make six half-inch slits in top.

Bake in 350 degree oven for one and one-half hours.
3 to 4 servings
October 26, 1975

Braised Duck

1 3- to 4-pound duck
1 tsp. salt
¼ tsp. pepper
2 T. fat
1 quart boiling water
1 medium onion, chopped
1 cup celery, chopped
1 cup carrot, chopped
2 cloves
1 bay leaf
2 T. parsley, chopped
1 T. all-purpose flour
1 T. butter, melted

Wash and dry duck thoroughly. Sprinkle with salt and pepper. Melt fat in large pan. Brown the duck on all sides over high heat. Add boiling water, onion, celery, carrot, cloves, bay leaf, and parsley. Cover and simmer until tender, about one and one-half hours. Remove the duck. Blend flour and butter and add to the pan liquid. Bring to a boil, stirring constantly.

Serve the duck on a hot platter with this gravy. (A mushroom sauce of your own choosing may be used instead of the gravy.)
3 to 4 servings
November 10, 1976

Duck in Grape Sauce

1 5-pound duck, cut in serving pieces
2 T. butter
½ clove garlic
2 T. all-purpose flour
1 cup grape juice
½ cup grape jelly
¼ cup mushrooms, chopped
2 sprigs parsley
pinch marjoram
salt, to taste
8 white onions
8 small carrots

Remove giblets from duck and coarsely chop. Brown duck in butter. Transfer to casserole. Crush garlic in buttered skillet; blend in flour. Pour in grape juice and add jelly, stirring to mix thoroughly. Drop in mushrooms, parsley, marjoram, and giblets and sprinkle with salt. In a casserole arrange onions and carrots around duck pieces. Pour sauce over all.

Cover and bake in a 350 degree oven for about one and a half hours.
4 servings
November 19, 1966

Duck with Barbecue Sauce

8 tsp. lemon juice
2 tsp. Worcestershire sauce
2 tsp. mustard
2 tsp. catsup
2 T. butter
4 large wild ducks
2 tsp. salt
1 tsp. paprika
brown sugar, as needed
2 medium apples, finely grated
   (optional)

Combine lemon juice, Worcestershire sauce, mustard, catsup and butter.

Cut breasts from ducks (8 pieces). Broil pieces until brown, about 15 minutes, basting continuously with barbecue sauce. After the meat starts browning, sprinkle with salt, paprika, brown sugar, and apple. Continue broiling for 45 minutes for well done meat.
8 servings
November 10, 1977

To Cook Wild Duck

Because wild duck is dry and has a strong taste, here is an excellent way of cooking it to moisten it and to draw out the strong taste:

Make a dressing of apples, carrots, onions and celery, and after removing all surplus fat from the birds, stuff them. Lay them breast down in the roaster, with a strip of bacon across backs. Pour boiling water over and cook slowly. One hour is usually enough for a young duck, and 2 hours for an old one. When done, remove dressing, turn birds breast side up and brown.

Some folks like to sprinkle a little resin in the duck feathers and pull them with the grain, rather than against as with chickens.
Prairie Farmer, November 10, 1934

5

How To Cook Your Goose

Long Form and Short Form. Does that make you think of taxes? Well guess what! The goose farmers of the country have something far nicer for you to think about and, while it involves a Long Form and a Short Form, the results are not only *not* painful, they're downright delicious.

The Long Form and the Short Form in this case have to do with how to roast a goose. If you have plenty of other things to do and don't want to be bothered with extra work, then listen to Herbert Ramsay, President of the National Goose Council. He'll tell you the bare bones way of preparing a roast goose, and if you follow his suggestions, you won't find yourself spending one unnecessary minute in the kitchen.

On the other hand, if cooking is recreation to you, if you pride yourself on producing the best gourmet results possible, then, oh boy, has the Goose Council got a recipe for you!

But let's start with Ramsay's recipe. It's shorter.

"On a Sunday morning, long about 7:30 A.M., take your defrosted goose from the refrigerator, remove it from its packaging, and lightly salt the body cavity. Put the bird in a roasting pan, stuff with a peeled onion, and shove it into a 400 degree oven. Leaven it there for about an hour while you're getting ready for church, and then turn the temperature down to 300 degrees. If you get back from church at about 11:00 A.M., you'll find that the bird is so tender that the meat will be falling off the bones. It's as easy as that."

The National Goose Council has some suggestions that are *not* as easy as that, but true gourmets and people who've spent their lives in the goose industry swear by these directions and recommend them to all of us.

1   Thaw in the refrigerator for a day or two depending on size, or for an hour a pound at room temperature, or for four to six hours in cold water.

2   *Preheat oven to 400 degrees.*

3   Remove the neck and giblets from the body cavity, and cook them promptly or refrigerate until ready to use.

4   Remove excess fat from the body cavity and neck skin. Reserve the fat and render it for use in other cooking. Rinse the bird and drain.

5   The wings may be removed at the second joint or tied flat against the body with a cord

around each wing and across the back. If the end pieces of wings are removed, cook them with the neck and giblets. If unstuffed, sprinkle the body cavity lightly with salt.

6 To stuff, fill the neck and body cavity loosely. Fasten the neck skin to the back with a skewer. Tie the legs together or tuck in the band of skin at the tail that you'll find with some birds.

7 Place the goose, breast side up, on a rack in a shallow roasting pan. Insert a meat thermometer deep into the inside thigh muscle.

8 Roast uncovered for 45 minutes to an hour, depending on the size of the bird, in the preheated oven. There is no need to baste the bird.

9 After roasting for 45 minutes to an hour, reduce the oven temperature to 325 degrees and continue roasting.

10 During roasting, spoon or siphon off the accumulated fat and reserve for use as shortening in other cooking. This should be done at half-hour intervals so that the fat doesn't brown excessively.

11 Roast until the thermometer registers 180 to 185 degrees.

12 If you're not using a thermometer, prick the thigh with a fork. The juices running out of the thigh should be beige in color, not pink. The skin should be golden brown and crisp.

So, which do you prefer? The Long or the Short Form? At least that's a more pleasant decision when the subject is roast goose rather than your taxes.

But why roast a goose—or stew it or braise it—for that matter? Just what has goose got going for it as a food?

Plenty, according to Herbert Ramsay. He's certain that if more of us tried this delectable bird, we'd like it enough to reverse a trend of fewer and fewer geese eaten in this country each year. "Geese," he claims, "have an exceptionally good flavor. The meat is succulent and distinctive. And when properly cooked, goose meat is one of the lowest in fat of all meats."

The fat in geese is almost all in a layer just underneath the skin. With proper roasting, most of it will render away, and the meat that's left is only 8 percent fat. "Slice into it," urges Ramsay, "and you'll see how lean it is."

The rendered fat needn't be wasted. It can be used to replace shortening in biscuits, pies, or cream sauces. "It's different from other animal fats," points out Ramsay, "because you can use it instead of shortening...something you couldn't do as successfully with, say, bacon grease or beef lard."

He says that since most geese we buy will be frozen, and since the goose should be thawed completely before cooking, it's worth knowing how to defrost it correctly. It all depends on how much time you have until you want to cook your goose.

To thaw in the refrigerator, leave a 6- to 10-pound bird in its original wrap on a tray for a day to a day and a half. For a 10- to 14-pound bird, allow a day and a half to two days.

To thaw the goose at room temperature, leave the frozen bird in its original wrap and place it in a brown paper bag or in a couple of layers of newspaper. Place it on a tray and allow about an hour a pound for thawing. Refrigerate it or cook it as soon as it's thawed.

And if you're in a hurry, you can safely speed the thawing process by placing the goose, still in its original wrap, in the sink with cold water. Change the water several times to hurry the thawing. A small goose, around 6 pounds, will be ready to cook in about 4 hours. A 14-pound bird should take about 6 hours.

Now roast your goose, according to the Long Form or the Short Form, or following the recipes collected here. But however you choose to cook it, be happy that you have something better to consider than income taxes.

Menu for Christmas Dinner

Roast Goose with Apple-Orange
*   *Stuffing**
Apple-Yam Scallop*
Steamed Broccoli
Jellied Cranberries*
Horns of Gold Rolls* and Butter
Crisp Green Salad
Cranberry Meringue Pudding* or
*   *Cranberry Crown Pie**
Milk
Coffee or Tea

*Recipes included

Roast Goose

1 or 2 geese (allow approximately
*   *¾ pound for each person you are*
*   *serving)*

Apple-Orange Stuffing:
6 cups day-old bread cubes
2 cups apples, diced
1 cup orange sections, diced
½ cup raisins
½ cup pecans, chopped
1 tsp. salt
½ tsp. poultry seasoning
½ cup orange juice
¼ cup melted fat

Combine all ingredients and toss lightly to mix.

Enough stuffing for 8- to 10-pound goose.

Lightly stuff goose with stuffing mixture. Roast goose according to the method described at the beginning of this chapter.

Allow the following approximate roasting times for a stuffed whole goose.

Bird weight	Total roasting time
6 - 8 lbs.	1¾ - 2¼ hrs.
8 - 10 lbs.	2¼ - 3 hrs.
10 - 12 lbs.	3 - 3½ hrs.
12 - 14 lbs.	3½ - 3¾ hrs.

Roast Goose

Scrub the goose on the outside, with warm water, as the skin is very dusty, on account of the oiliness, which holds the dust that sifts through the feathers. Wash the inside quickly, rinse and wipe it. Be careful to save all the extra fat to try out, as goose grease is invaluable as a remedy for colds or soreness in the chest. Fill the body and breast with the following dressing. Be careful not to fill it too full, but allow room for the dressing to swell.
Wisconsin Farmer,
December 12, 1912

Apple-Yam Scallop

4 large sweet potatoes (may use
   canned)
4 tart apples, pared and cored
butter, as needed
brown sugar, as needed
nutmeg, as desired

Bake or boil sweet potatoes until tender, peel, and cut into one-half-inch thick slices. Cut apples into thin slices. Arrange alternate layers of sweet potatoes and apples in buttered baking dish. Sprinkle each layer with brown sugar and dash of nutmeg. Dot with butter.

Bake covered in 350 degree oven for 30-35 minutes. Serve immediately.
6 servings
December, 1970

Jellied Cranberries

1½ cups water
1½ cups sugar
1 pound cranberries

Cook sugar and water together until sugar is dissolved and water is boiling rapidly. Add washed cranberries and cook three to four minutes until popping ceases. Pour into oiled mold; chill. This makes a stiff cranberry mold that looks nice on the plate.
November 19, 1955

Horn of Gold Rolls

2 packages active dry yeast
¼ cup warm water, 110-115 degrees
½ cup sugar
½ cup shortening, part butter
2 eggs
1 tsp. salt
½ cup scalded milk
4 cups sifted all-purpose flour

Add the yeast to warm water and let stand. Measure into a large bowl the sugar, shortening, eggs, and salt. Beat until smooth.

Blend in the scalded milk. Stir yeast mixture well. Add to the milk mixture in the bowl, beating until smooth. Mix in the flour, blending again until smooth. Scrape dough from sides of bowl.

Cover bowl with foil, let rise in warm place about one and one-half hours, or until doubled.

Turn dough out on lightly floured board. Shape one-fourth of the dough at a time, keeping the rest covered. Roll out one part into an eight-inch circle, about one-quarter inch thick. Cut into eight pie-shaped pieces. To shape horns, roll each piece of dough from the wide side toward the point, stretching slightly as you roll. Place on baking sheet about one inch apart, curling ends. Continue shaping all the dough. Cover with damp cloth, then a dry one, and let rise in warm place for about one hour, or until doubled. Cloth should be damp to prevent sticking.

Preheat oven to 400 degrees. Bake rolls 10 to 15 minutes or until golden brown. Cool and brush with butter.

Dough may be chilled two to twenty-four hours before using.
November 15, 1969

The housewife who likes a touch of decoration will find a hint in the following: "The mantlepiece was banked with ears of red and yellow corn, ripe apples, nuts and other fruits of the harvest. Christmas ferns, bittersweet, ground pine and the scarlet berries of the fire bush were the floral trophies. The centerpiece was a large pumpkin, hollowed out to make a basket, and in this were heaped the fruits that were to be served at the close of the dinner."
The Wisconsin Farmer, November 21, 1901

Cranberry Meringue Pudding

½ cup all-purpose flour, sifted
2 tsp. baking powder
1 cup sugar
¼ tsp. salt
2 egg yolks
2 T. butter, melted
2 cups cranberries, chopped
½ cup dates, chopped
½ cup nuts, chopped

Meringue:
2 egg whites
6 T. sugar
¼ tsp. salt
½ tsp. lemon extract

Sift flour, baking powder, sugar, and salt together. Beat egg yolks, reserving whites for the meringue. Add egg yolks, butter, cranberries, dates, and nuts to flour mixture. Mix well. Spread in an oiled cake pan 8×8×2 inches.

Bake in a 350 degree oven about 30 minutes.

Prepare meringue by beating egg whites until frothy; add salt and lemon extract. Beat until stiff, but not dry. Add sugar gradually and beat until stiff. Spread meringue over pudding. Continue baking 12 to 15 minutes or until meringue is delicately brown. Cut in squares to serve, either hot or cold.

9 servings
November 15, 1941

Here's the perfect end to a Christmas meal.

Cranberry Crown Pie

2½ cups sugar
½ cup water
2 cups apple, chopped
4 cups cranberries
juice and grated rind of ½ orange
2 T. cornstarch
2 T. cold water
one-crust pastry for 10-inch pie,
    cooked and cooled
2 egg whites
¼ cup sugar
2 T. almonds, slivered (optional)

Combine two and one-half cups sugar, water, apple, cranberries, and orange rind and juice in a saucepan. Cook mixture rapidly about 10 minutes, or until cranberries pop. Make a paste of the cornstarch and cold water; stir into hot fruit mixture. Cook an additional five minutes, or until mixture is thickened and clear.

Fill pastry crust with fruit mixture.

Prepare meringue by beating egg whites until stiff; add one-quarter cup sugar gradually, beating constantly until meringue is thick, but not dry. Pile in a ring around the edge of the pie and scatter with almonds, if used.

Bake in a 325 degree oven about 15 minutes, or until meringue is golden.

6 servings
November 16, 1957

Applesauce for Roast Goose

Apples should always accompany goose and pork. You may serve a good applesauce or peel some fine ones and cut into quarters, removing the cores. Make a sirup of a cupful of sugar and a cupful of water, letting it cook five minutes; then drop in the apples. Cook until transparent, but do not let them break; remove to a dish, boil down the sirup and pour over them. Bits of lemon peel may be added if liked.

January 6, 1910

Mock Goose

Wipe an eight to 10 pound leg of pork with a damp cloth. Place on rack in roaster; add one cup water. Cover roaster and roast one hour in a 375 degree Fahrenheit or moderate oven. Then remove skin by making an incision in it, cutting through to the end of the shank. Grasp skin at cut end, using a cloth or fork and with one quick jerk, remove the entire skin in one piece. Rub the fat with one-half teaspoon dried mustard, sprinkle with powdered sage, pepper, salt, bread crumbs and finely minced onion and green pepper. Dust lightly with brown sugar. Return to oven and continue baking, increasing the fire to 375 degrees Fahrenheit. Baste frequently, allowing 20 to 25 minutes to the pound. An eight-pound roast will require about three hours to roast. Serve with gooseberry jam or tart apple sauce.
September 29, 1927

Old-fashioned Goose Giblets and Barley Soup

*2 T. rendered goose fat (use drippings
  from roasting goose) or butter
1 cup onion, sliced
goose giblets, neck, and carcass
5 cups water
1 tsp. salt
½ tsp. celery salt
1 can (1 pound) tomatoes, cut up
1 cup pearl barley
1 tsp. beef stock base
½ tsp. thyme*

Melt fat in a Dutch oven or large kettle. Saute onion until limp but not browned. Add giblets, neck, carcass, water, salt, and celery salt. Bring to a boil. Reduce heat, cover and simmer one hour. Remove meat and bones with a slotted spoon. Cut meat off neck and carcass and finely chop giblets; return meat to kettle. If desired, add leftover cut-up roast goose. Add tomatoes, barley, beef base, and thyme. Return to a boil, cover, and simmer one additional hour.
2 quarts

Fricasseed Goose with Potato Dumplings

Stew:
*goose back, wings, neck, giblets, and
  heart
½ tsp. salt
¼ tsp. pepper
¼ tsp. ginger
6 cups water
1 cup onion, sliced
2 stalks celery, with tops, cut up
1 clove garlic, crushed
2 tsp. chicken seasoned stock base
1 tsp. salt
4 T. rendered goose fat (use drippings
  from roasting goose)
⅓ cup butter
⅓ cup all-purpose flour
1 package (10-ounce) frozen peas
  and carrots*

In a Dutch oven or large kettle place goose back, wings, neck, giblets, and heart with one-half teaspoon salt, pepper, and ginger. Cover with water. Add onion, celery, garlic, stock base, and one teaspoon salt. Bring to a boil. Cover, reduce heat, and simmer for two hours, stirring occasionally. Strain into a bowl.

In a Dutch oven melt goose fat and butter. Blend in flour, stirring to make a smooth paste. Gradually add strained broth, stirring until smooth. Remove meat from bones; cut up giblets and heart; return to kettle. (Add any leftover roast goose, cut up.) Add vegetables. Bring to a boil; cover, reduce heat, and simmer 15 minutes.

Prepare Potato Dumplings.

Potato Dumplings:

1 cup mashed potatoes
1 egg, beaten
½ cup all-purpose flour
½ tsp. dried parsley flakes
¼ tsp. salt
dash of nutmeg

Combine potatoes, egg, flour, parsley, salt, and nutmeg. Stir with a fork until well blended. Drop by tablespoonsful onto boiling stew. When dumplings rise to the surface, cover and simmer 12 to 15 minutes. To test for doneness, remove one dumpling and separate with two forks.

To serve, spoon dumplings into large soup bowls. Ladle goose mixture over dumplings.

6 servings, with two dumplings each

Late Autumn is a special time of the year. It's that pause between the crisp days of October, with blue skies contrasted against the brilliant fall foliage, and the shorter days and gray skies of later November reminding us that winter will soon be here. From inside the house come the wonderful aromas of meat roasting and stews simmering. It's a good time to get back to the hearty fall and winter meals.

You're lucky indeed if you have a supply of wild game. For the cook concerned about cost, nutrition, and good taste, game gets a high score on all three points. And here's a tempting way to cook your wild goose:

Wild Goose

1 wild goose
1 T. salt
1 T. baking soda
2 pounds cooking apples, sliced
1 cup raisins
4 stalks celery
salt and pepper, as desired
3 strips bacon
1 small onion
3 T. shortening
½ cup water

Soak bird, whether frozen or fresh, in cold water with salt and baking soda for two hours. Pat dry and stuff with apples and raisins. Close up opening with toothpicks. Place in shallow pan, breast up, and season well. Slice stalks of celery and onion into bottom of pan. Place bacon on breast of bird. Put water and shortening into bottom of pan.

Cook in a 325 degree oven, uncovered first hour, covered the second hour. Remove cover the third hour and baste every 20 minutes. Add water if necessary. Baste the last half hour with wild duck glaze. Pan will be browned for making gravy when finished.

Glaze:

½ cup butter
1 cup burgundy
1 cup current jelly

Combine ingredients. Bring to a boil for a minute or so, then use to baste goose.

6 servings
November 5, 1977

Once the goose is roasted, be sure to save a few slices of meat for this favorite from the 50s.

Goosepuff Casserole

1 chicken bouillon cube
1 cup hot water
1 cup milk
4 slices onion
4 T. butter
¼ cup all-purpose flour
1 cup (¼ pound) sharp cheddar
   cheese, grated
8 to 10 slices cooked goose
¼ tsp. salt
⅛ pepper
4 slices bread

Dissolve bouillon cube in hot water. Add milk and onion. In a medium sized saucepan, melt butter; blend in flour and cook slowly until frothy. Add milk mixture all at once. Cook, stirring until thickened throughout. Lift out onion. Blend three-quarters of the cheese into the sauce.

Lightly butter four shallow, individual casseroles (about three-quarter-cup capacity). Place goose slices in each. (Or use a single nine-inch glass pie plate.) If desired, sprinkle with salt and pepper. Pour about one-quarter of the sauce over goose slices and top with bread. Pour remaining sauce over to completely cover bread. Top with remaining cheese.

Bake in a 325 degree oven for 45 minutes to an hour, or until sauce is bubbly and the top is nicely browned. Serve promptly.
4 servings
December 19, 1959

6

With Pheasants, Unisex Is the Shape of the Future

 If you're a pheasant hunter or a pheasant eater, read on. We'll be discussing what could be the shape of the future.

And if you're neither, read on anyway. You'll have a chance to learn how modern science is helping to increase our stock of game birds. The fact is, there's something special going on in the pheasant world and it revolves around a pheasant you may never have heard of—the Melanistic pheasant.

If there were a *Vogue* magazine for pheasants, the Melanistic pheasant could very well be on one of the covers. People who care about game birds would recognize this bird as one with the style and shape and color that it takes to be really "in."

Probably the biggest thing in its favor is a good, 1980s style unisex look.

"But why," you may ask, "would unisex be important to anyone but a few, trendy fashion designers?"

Jack Krout from Krout's Pheasant Farm can explain. As a pheasant breeder, he knows that with pheasants, a unisex look can mean far better utilization of resources. Let's visit him at his Petaluma, California, farm and find out why.

He's standing beside a 6 by 12 foot chicken wire cage that contains two unusual looking pheasants—they're both totally black. We watch as they contentedly peck corn and soybean meal from the ground.

"If you were the manager of a hunting club," Krout begins, "you'd find that almost all hunters prefer the large, colorful male pheasants. As the club manager, you'd find that at the end of the season, you'd have too many females and not enough males." He turns slightly to face another cage, one that's near the Melanistic pheasants. "Here's what I mean. Look at the male Ring Neck pheasant," he says, pointing to a brilliantly colored bird. "Notice how big the bird is and how bright the plumage is compared to the females?"

He's right. The male is a third again the size of the females, and its tail feathers extend nearly two feet. The colors are truly brilliant. The females, in contrast, are drab grayish tan and their tail feathers couldn't be more than nine or ten inches long. The male would make a far more attractive prize, not to mention a bigger dinner.

"This difference between the sexes is normal throughout most of the pheasant world," explains Krout, "and there's a reason for it. When the hen pheasant is sitting on her eggs, she's hard to notice. The male, being colorful and big, can draw the attention of predators away from his mate, and that helps insure the survival of the species."

Krout turns back toward the Melanistic pheasants. "Notice," he continues, pointing to the Melanistic female, "that she's almost the same size and color as the male? If you were hunting, you couldn't tell whether you had a male or a female in your gun's sight. Since you'd be taking birds of either sex, there's a better balance and a more efficient utilization of resources."

You may not find the Melanistic pheasants in your licensed hunting club right away, and, like other things having to do with fashion and taste, they may not catch on. But whether they do or not, pheasant breeders are working to insure better utilization of our wildlife resources.

Whether a Melanistic pheasant or a more traditional one, Jack Krout and his wife, Verna, know a lot about how to cook them. Let's move inside to the kitchen, where Verna Krout is about to prepare dinner.

She walks to the refrigerator and takes out two plucked pheasants. "It's a good idea to age a bird three or four days before eating it," she says. "These pheasants have been in the refrigerator four days, and they'll be noticeably more tender and flavorful today than they would have been if I had cooked them the first day."

While she's drying one of the birds with paper towelling, Verna remarks, "I've cooked a lot of birds, and if you like, I'll share one of the most useful tips I know. It's that a frozen bird can keep its quality surprisingly well if you wrap it right. Watch how I do it.

"First," she says, "makes sure that the bird is completely dry so that no ice crystals can form between the bird and the bag. Then put the bird in a freezer bag, and make sure that there are no pockets of air." Using her palms and fingers, she presses as much air from the plastic bag as she can. Next, she inserts a drinking straw into the plastic bag and, sucking the remaining air from the bag, makes the heavy plastic cling to the pheasant like another layer of skin.

"It's worth going to this extra trouble because any air in the wrapper can cause freezer burn. In fact, to be sure that you're not going to get little tears in the plastic as you rummage around in the freezer and jostle the bags, overwrap the plastic with freezer paper or foil."

Now to the most important question—how is she going to cook the remaining pheasant?

"I like to stuff game birds with bourbon-soaked dried fruits like these." With her fingers, she fishes out a few prunes and apricots from a jar that smells of bourbon, and inserts them in the pheasant cavity, followed by a few apple slices and several chunks of celery. Then she rubs the breast and legs with butter, and puts the bird into a roasting pan. Finally, it's into the oven, at 375 degrees.

"It'll be ready to eat in about an hour and a half. I'll baste it every 10 to 15 minutes to keep it from drying out. And it will be delicious!"

As the recipes that follow will also be.

Menu for a Hearty Pheasant Dinner

Royal Pheasant*
Steamed Rice
Fresh Cranberry-Orange Mold*
Lemon Parsley Carrots*
Mincemeat Tarts*
Coffee or Tea

*Recipe included

Royal Pheasant

1 pheasant, cut into serving pieces
all-purpose flour, as needed
butter, as needed
salt and pepper, to taste
1 onion, grated
¼ pound mushrooms, sliced
1 can cream of mushroom soup
½ cup sherry
½ pint sour cream

Dredge pheasant in flour; brown in butter. Place in a casserole; season with salt and pepper. Cover with onion, mushrooms, soup, sherry, and sour cream.

Cover casserole and bake in a 350 degree oven until tender, about 60 minutes. 2 to 3 servings (Double recipe for dinner serving four people.)

Lemon Parsley Carrots

¾ cup water
1 bunch carrots, sliced into ¼-inch
    rounds (about 3 cups)
½ tsp. salt
½ tsp. lemon peel, freshly grated
2 T. lemon juice, freshly squeezed
1 T. sugar
1 T. fresh parsley, snipped
2 T. butter

In saucepan bring water to a boil; add carrots and salt. Cook covered for 10 to 15 minutes or until just tender; drain well. In saucepan combine remaining ingredients, heat until butter is melted and sugar is dissolved. Add drained carrots and toss like a salad to mix. Serve at once.
4 servings
September 4, 1971

Fresh Cranberry-Orange Mold

4 cups cranberries
2 oranges, quartered with seeds
    removed
2 cups sugar
1 package cherry-flavored gelatin
1¼ cup boiling water

Put cranberries and oranges, including rind, through a food grinder, using a coarse blade. Stir in sugar and chill.*

To prepare salad mold, dissolve gelatin in boiling water; chill until gelatin is partially set. Add cranberry-orange mixture. Pour into oiled one-quart mold or six to eight individual molds. Chill until firm.

*This mixture makes a relish which will keep for weeks when stored in the refrigerator.
6 to 8 servings
November 21, 1959

Mincemeat Tarts

2 cups sifted all-purpose flour
1 tsp. salt
⅔ cup shortening
3 to 5 T. cold water
1½ cups mincemeat

Preheat oven to 450 degrees.

Sift together flour and salt. Cut or rub in shortening. Add cold water, and mix to a dry, crumbly dough. Toss onto a lightly floured pastry cloth. Press the dough together. Roll out to one-eighth-inch thickness. Cut twelve three-inch scalloped rounds and twelve two and one-half-inch doughnut rounds. Place the scalloped rounds on an ungreased baking sheet. Put two tablespoons of mincemeat on each of the rounds. Top with the doughnut rounds, and seal the edges together.

Bake in oven for 12 to 15 minutes.
12 tarts, or 4 to 6 servings
December 20, 1947

Jack's Barbecued Pheasant Teriyaki

½ cup soy sauce
½ cup green Hungarian wine (or any semi-dry, fruity wine)
4 T. wildflower honey
1 tsp. ginger
2 T. fresh orange juice
2 tsp. fresh lemon juice
1 pheasant, cut in halves
salt and pepper, to taste

Combine soy sauce, wine, honey, and ginger. Heat slightly to blend. Add orange and lemon juice. Place pheasant in a shallow glass baking dish, pour the above marinade over it, and let it stand in the refrigerator for four or more hours.

Broil over a medium hot charcoal fire, turning and basting frequently with the marinade. Cook until the leg bones turn easily, about 35 to 40 minutes.

Season lightly to taste with salt and pepper.

2 to 3 servings
Source: Krout's Pheasant Farm

Krout's Easy and Elegant Pheasant

1 pheasant, whole or halved
¼ cup butter
1 cup sliced fresh mushrooms, or 1 cup canned mushrooms
½ cup chicken or pheasant stock or broth
½ cup white wine
2 T. scallions, chopped
2 T. parsley, chopped
all-purpose flour, as needed

Brown pheasant in butter over medium heat until golden. Remove bird to a casserole with a cover. If using fresh mushrooms, brown lightly in the same skillet, add stock, wine, scallions, and parsley, and let simmer a few minutes. Pour over pheasant. (If using canned mushrooms, add them to pheasant with broth, wine, scallions, and parsley.)

Cover casserole and bake in 350 degree oven for one hour and 15 minutes, or until leg joints move easily. May be uncovered for last 20 minutes or so. Remove extra fat, then thicken sauce with flour.

Good served with rice pilaf or wild rice and a nice white wine.

2 to 3 servings
Source: Krout's Pheasant Farm

Pheasant Baked in Beer

2 to 3 pheasants, cut in serving pieces
pancake flour, as needed
salt and pepper, to taste
shortening, as needed
2 to 3 cups beer

Roll pheasant pieces in pancake flour, season with salt and pepper, and brown on all sides in hot fat. Put in roaster; add beer.

Roast in a 300 degree oven for one and a half hours. Increase heat to 350 degrees and roast another one and a half hours, basting every half hour.

January 9, 1971

Crispy Braised Pheasant

1 pheasant, cut in serving pieces
seasoned all-purpose flour, as needed
¼ cup butter
1 cup mushrooms, sliced
3 T. onion, chopped
1 chicken bouillon cube
½ cup hot water
1 T. lemon juice
½ tsp. salt
⅛ tsp. pepper

Roll pheasant pieces in flour; brown in butter for about 10 minutes, or until golden brown. Remove pheasant, add mushrooms and onion and cook until golden brown. Return meat to skillet; dissolve bouillon cube in water; add bouillon, lemon juice, salt, and pepper. Cover and simmer one hour, or until tender; remove cover during last 10 or 15 minutes of cooking time to recrisp meat.

This is a good method for cooking older birds; suitable for younger birds, also.
4 servings
November 2, 1963

Barbecued Pheasant

1 young pheasant
¼ to ½ tsp. salt
⅛ tsp. pepper
melted butter, as needed
barbecue sauce (commercial or your
favorite)

Cut pheasant in pieces. Using a sharp knife, cut meat from each side of breast bone. Sprinkle each piece with salt and pepper. Brush well with melted butter.

Line the bottom of a broiling pan with foil. Flatten pheasant pieces on foil. Broil slowly with meat seven to nine inches from heat. Turn occasionally and baste with barbecue sauce. Broil until tender, about 30 to 40 minutes.
4 servings
November 2, 1963

Deep Fried Pheasant Four Ways

For 1 young pheasant:
¼ cup coating mixture*
milk or buttermilk, as needed
cooking oil

*Coating mixtures:
1 *¼ cup all-purpose flour*
   1 tsp. paprika
   ¾ tsp. salt
   ⅛ tsp. pepper

2 *¼ cup pancake mix*
   ¼ tsp. salt

3 *¼ cup all-purpose flour*
   ¾ tsp. salt
   ¼ tsp. pepper
   ¹⁄₁₆ tsp. oregano
   ¹⁄₁₆ tsp. basil

4 *1 egg, slightly beaten*
   ½ cup milk
   ½ cup all-purpose flour
   ½ to 1 tsp. Worcestershire sauce
   ⅛ tsp. allspice
   ¼ tsp. salt
   ⅛ tsp. pepper

Combine ingredients in desired coating mixture and beat with a rotary beater until smooth.

Cut meat from each side of breast-bone with a sharp knife, making two breast pieces. Marinate in milk or buttermilk one to two hours in the refrigerator, or dip in milk. Dredge pieces in coating mixture. Dry on rack approximately 30 minutes.

Preheat oil in deep fat fryer to 350 to 360 degrees. Transfer a few coated pheasant pieces at a time to the frying basket and lower into oil. Use two inches or more of oil. Fry for three to five minutes, or until golden brown. Remove and serve immediately. (If you are preparing a large quantity of pheasant, keep fried pieces hot in a single layer in a flat casserole in a 300 degree oven.)
2 servings
November 10, 1974

Pheasant with Cabbage

½ cup onion, chopped
½ cup cabbage, chopped
1 egg, lightly beaten
¼ tsp. salt
⅛ tsp. pepper
2 T. milk
1 slice bread, cubed, or ½ cup
    bread crumbs
1 young pheasant
8 slices bacon

Preheat oven to 400 degrees.

Combine onion, cabbage, egg, salt, pepper, milk, and bread to make a wet dressing. Stuff cavity of bird. Close openings with string and skewers or toothpicks. Completely cover breast and all meaty portions of bird with bacon. Tie in place.

Place bird, breast side up, on rack in shallow roasting pan. Roast in oven until tender, about 50 to 60 minutes.

Promptly remove dressing from bird.
4 servings
November 10, 1974

Pheasant Baked in Onion Rings

1 young pheasant, cut in serving pieces
¼ cup seasoned all-purpose flour
1 large onion, sliced in rings
¼ cup butter, melted
1 T. lemon juice
1 tsp. Worcestershire sauce
salt and pepper, to taste

Roll pheasant in flour. Arrange dredged pieces in an oiled shallow casserole. Cover pheasant pieces with onion rings. Pour butter over. Sprinkle with lemon juice, Worcestershire, salt, and pepper.

Bake in a 375 degree oven until tender, about one hour. If more browning is desired, set oven up to 450 degrees for the last 15 minutes.
4 servings
November 19, 1960

Pheasant in Cream

1 pheasant, cut in serving pieces
¼ cup all-purpose flour
¾ tsp. salt
⅛ tsp. paprika
½ cup sour or sweet cream
¼ cup cooking fat
1 3½-ounce can mushrooms (optional)
2 T. onion, chopped

Mix flour, salt, and paprika. Dredge meat in seasoned flour. If convenient, allow to dry on rack for about a half hour. Heat one-quarter-inch cooking fat in skillet. Brown the pheasant pieces evenly and slowly, avoid piercing the coating. Allow 15 or 20 minutes for browning. Remove pieces and place one layer deep in a shallow casserole. Brown the mushrooms and onion in fat in skillet. Cover pheasant pieces with mushroom and onion mixture. Drizzle two tablespoons of sour (or sweet) cream over each browned piece of pheasant in the casserole.

Bake in a 350 degree oven for 45 to 60 minutes or until forktender. Do not cover a young bird. An older bird may be baked until tender, then uncovered and baked until crisp. Add more cream if meat gets dry.
4 servings
November 19, 1960

Braised Herb Pheasant

2½ cups milk
1 pheasant, about 2½ pounds, washed
and cut into 4 portions
21 round buttery crackers, finely rolled
(about ¾ cup crumbs)
½ cup butter
4 pearl onions, parboiled 4 to 5
minutes
½ pound fresh mushrooms, sliced
3 T. all-purpose flour
1½ tsp. salt
¼ tsp. white pepper
½ tsp. ground sage
¼ tsp. ground thyme
⅛ tsp. nutmeg
2 T. parsley, chopped
pitted dates, as needed
bacon slices as needed, cut in half

Pour one-quarter cup of milk into a shallow dish; dip pheasant in milk, then in crumbs. Heat one-quarter cup butter in large skillet; brown pheasant slowly on both sides. Transfer to an 11¾×7½×1¾-inch baking dish. Arrange onions and mushrooms on top.

Melt remaining butter in a separate saucepan; blend in flour, salt, pepper, sage, thyme and nutmeg; cook one minute. Gradually add remaining milk. Bring to a boil, stirring constantly. Pour over pheasant and vegetables. Cover.

Bake in a 275 degree oven for two hours. Remove cover; sprinkle parsley on top. Allowing three to four per person, wrap dates in bacon slices; cook slowly in skillet, turning to brown evenly. Place around casserole.

4 servings (about 6 ounces pheasant and ½ cup sauce)
October 22, 1977

Pheasant Kiev

2 pheasant breasts, halved and boned
¼ pound butter, softened
1 tsp. parsley, finely chopped
1 small garlic clove, crushed and
finely chopped
few grains cayenne pepper
¾ cup all-purpose flour
1 egg, beaten
1½ cups dry bread crumbs or cornflake crumbs
vegetable oil for deep fat frying
hot cooked rice, as needed

Place each of the four half-breasts between waxed paper and flatten with a wooden mallet to one-half-inch thickness. Be careful not to break holes in the meat. Place the thin fillets in the refrigerator for two hours.

Mix the parsley, garlic, and cayenne with the softened butter and shape the butter into four egg-shaped balls. Place the butter in the freezer until the pheasant is chilled.

After two hours, remove pheasant fillets from refrigerator and brush one side of each with beaten egg. Place a piece of butter on the egg-coated side of each fillet and fold the meat over it to make an envelope. Secure the edges with toothpicks. Roll each fillet in flour, dip into beaten egg, and then roll it in bread crumbs.

Heat oil to 375 degrees in a deep fat fryer. Carefully place the fillets in a frying basket and lower into the hot fat. Cook seven to eight minutes or until golden brown.

Serve immediately with rice.
4 servings
October 22, 1977

Braised Pheasant

2 pheasants, cut in serving pieces
¼ cup seasoned all-purpose flour
4 T. shortening
4 cups chicken consomme
6 T. butter
1 pound mushrooms, sliced
½ cup sour cream

Shake pheasant pieces in seasoned flour in a paper bag. Brown in shortening. Place in heavy baking dish or roaster and add consomme. The birds should be three-quarters submerged.

Simmer on top of the stove or braise in a 350 degree oven for one and a half hours, or until tender. Saute mushrooms in butter and add. Stir in sour cream fifteen minutes before serving.

4 servings
November 5, 1977

Hot Orange Sauce for Pheasant or Duck

¼ cup butter
¼ cup all-purpose flour
½ tsp. salt
1⅓ cups brown stock
1 cup orange juice
grated rind of 1 orange

Melt butter, add flour and salt, stirring until well-browned. Slowly add stock.

Just before serving with a roasted bird, add orange juice and orange rind. Pour over bird.

Sauce for one pheasant or duck—also good with squirrel.

November 2, 1963

7

The Right Stuff—For Stuffings

Recipes for cooking poultry have changed a lot in the last century. You'll no longer find directions like this one from the December 1911 issue of *The Wisconsin Farmer* that begins: "Singe [the bird] over a burning newspaper on a hot stove."

Being able to buy poultry that's ready for the oven is a major change that has occurred since great-grandmother's time—but it probably isn't the most important. A vital new ingredient in our poultry cooking is an understanding of food safety. With a few simple precautions, our food today can be more convenient than it ever was in the past, and it can also be safer.

The fact is, food poisoning was and is a common danger if you don't know the modern techniques for avoiding it. As Kathryn Boor, a Research Associate with Cooperative Extension at the University of California at Davis, explains, "Food poisoning is really very, very common. But," she's quick to add, "you may not get severely sick with it. More likely it's a mild case leaving you with a queasy feeling or cramps or maybe you just feel a little below par the next day. . .and never quite know why."

Fortunately Boor and other food technologists can tell us how to prevent the growth of the staphlococci and salmonella bacteria that cause food poisoning. "These bacteria," explains Boor, "grow most rapidly at temperatures between 50 and 140 degrees." That means to keep foods safe, we should maintain them at temperatures either below 40 degrees or above 140 degrees.

Boor has an immediate example of where we could get into trouble. "Let's say you're slow-roasting a 25-pound turkey at 200 degrees with two pounds of stuffing," she says. "The stuffing in the center may take too long to get out of the danger zone of 50 to 140 degrees."

When Boor says, "too long," she's referring to the fact that in just four hours at the wrong temperature, staphlococci germs can produce enough toxins to make you ill. "Toxins produced by staphlococci bacteria," she explains, "are not destroyed by normal cooking temperatures. The best strategy is to prevent their growth in the first place." That means, when you're slow-cooking poultry, cook the stuffing separately so that it won't be insulated by the turkey's body.

"Or, to pick another example," she continues, "you refrigerate the bird after you've cooked it, leaving the stuffing inside. Again, it may not cool down far enough and fast enough for you to eliminate the danger of spoilage." To avoid this problem, remove the stuffing from the bird and store it in a separate, covered container. The heat transfer is more efficient this way than if the stuffing were insulated inside the bird.

Here are some additional precautions that she recommends for maximizing food safety.

- If you've been handling raw poultry, wash your hands before touching the stuffing mixture. Food poisoning bacteria may not be destroyed when the stuffing is cooked inside the bird.

- Clean your cutting board and utensils after preparing your turkey and before preparing the stuffing. A plastic cutting board is preferable since it doesn't harbor bacteria as readily as wood. A wooden one will do, however, if you give it a quick scrub with detergent and your sink brush. As an added precaution, occasionally scrub your board with a diluted chlorine solution.

- Stuff your bird just before putting it in the oven—not earlier.

- Store leftover, cooked stuffing separately from the bird. Again, do this so that the temperature of the stuffing will quickly drop to 40 degrees or lower.

Safety is an important consideration, but it's certainly not the only one. Ms. Boor also has some tips on getting the best flavor from your stuffings. "The best stuffings are made the night before. This gives the flavors a chance to get to know each other. It's the same thing that happens to your favorite stew—you know how it always tastes better the next day?" Try making your

stuffing the night before, but be careful, she reminds us, to keep it refrigerated until you're going to cook it.

What about the ingredients? To avoid soggy stuffing, the bread should be a couple of days old. For special flavor, toast the cubes lightly.

If you're using a commercial stuffing mix, and if you don't use it all at once, you can safely store the rest of the package on your pantry shelf for a couple of months. The trick is to keep it in a vapor resistant container. This could be a mason jar with the lid screwed on tight, or it could be a sealed plastic bag.

The reason to keep the bread crumbs in a sealed container is to retard staleness. Flavor and texture deteriorate slightly as the crumbs age. "They're not unsafe," says Boor, "just not as good as they could be."

How does an expert like Boor make stuffings when she's doing the cooking? "Frankly," she admits, "I'm likely to put in whatever I have handy—celery, green pepper, onion, garlic. But here's the basic recipe. I cook the giblets in highly peppered water, about half a teaspoon per cup of water, and I add a pinch or two of sage." She pays special attention to the liver, which only requires about five minutes of gentle simmering before it's done. She's careful to remove it as soon as it's cooked because otherwise it will get hard and bitter. She simmers the heart, gizzard, and neck until they're tender, one to three hours, depending on the size of the bird.

"When they're done," she continues, "I chop the giblets along with some mushrooms, and add them all to about four cups of bread crumbs, along with maybe a quarter or half cup of melted butter. I'll add enough of the liquid from the giblets to moisten the bread crumbs. They should stick together but not 'glump.'

"I try to get this far the night before, and then refrigerate the stuffing in a covered ovenproof dish so that the flavors can blend. The next day, when it's time to cook the turkey or other bird, I'll take the dish from the refrigerator to the oven, and cook the stuffing, uncovered, at 375 degrees for about 45 minutes.

"As the stuffing cooks," Boor points out, "the flavors blend, the bread loses some of its moisture, and as it browns—that's a reaction between the sugars in the bread and the proteins— the flavor improves. I try to keep an eye on it to make sure the stuffing doesn't dry out. I'll add a little more water if it seems about to, and I'll definitely add more water if I'm reheating it another day."

Boor's recipe probably isn't too different from her own grandmother's. But is has one advantage that would be hard to put a price on: by always keeping it either quite hot or quite cold, Boor knows her food is not only tasty, but safe and healthy as well.

Old-fashioned Bread Stuffing

1½ cups onion, finely chopped
1½ cups celery, finely chopped
⅓ cup butter
8 cups dry bread cubes (½ inch)
1½ tsp. salt
⅛ tsp. pepper
½ tsp. poultry seasoning
½ tsp. sage
¼ cup water or broth
1 egg, well beaten

Saute onion and celery in butter in skillet until tender. Add mixture to bread cubes which have been placed in a large pan. Sprinkle with seasonings that have been mixed together. Combine. Add water or broth and egg. Toss together with forks.
9 cups stuffing, enough for a 12-pound bird
November 12, 1977

You might wish to experiment with these variations. Add to basic recipe.

Sausage Poultry Stuffing. Pan fry 2 lbs. sausage until brown and well cooked. Drain well.

Oyster Stuffing. Brown giblets from 1 turkey and 3 T. minced onion in butter. Substitute oyster liquor for water or broth. Add 1 pint chopped oysters and enough water, liquor, or broth to moisten slightly.

Cornbread Stuffing. Add 2 cups unsweetened cornbread, coarsely crumbled, to 6 cups bread cubes or herb-seasoned croutons.

Rice and Wheat Stuffing

2 cups cooked rice
1½ cups shredded wheat biscuits
¾ cup hot chicken bouillon or stock
¼ cup celery, finely chopped
2 T. green pepper, finely chopped
2 T. onion, finely chopped
¼ cup butter
2 T. parsley, minced
½ tsp. salt
½ tsp. poultry seasoning
¼ tsp. ground thyme
⅛ tsp. pepper

Mix together rice, wheat biscuits, and bouillon. Cook celery, green pepper, and onion in butter until tender. Add to rice mixture with parsley and seasonings.

Stuff bird. Alternately, you may bake in a covered casserole in a 350 degree oven for 20 minutes. Uncover. Bake 10 minutes longer, or until brown.
4 cups stuffing, or enough for a four pound bird
November 11, 1967

Almond-Bran Stuffing for Chicken

2 cups fortified whole bran cereal
¾ cup toasted almonds, slivered
½ cup celery, chopped
¼ cup onion, finely chopped
¼ cup parsley, chopped
1 tsp. grated lemon rind
½ tsp. salt
¼ tsp. pepper
¼ tsp. crushed rosemary leaves
¼ tsp. poultry seasoning
⅓ cup butter, melted

Combine all ingredients except butter. Toss with melted butter until well mixed.
Stuffing for one 5- to 5½-pound chicken
December, 1976

Rice-Water Chestnut Stuffing

1 large onion, chopped
½ cup (1 stick) butter
¼ cup parsley, chopped
2 cups green grapes, halved
½ cup orange juice
4 cups cooked rice
2 tsp. salt
1 cup water chestnuts, sliced
½ cup pecans, chopped
½ cup dried apricots, chopped

Cook onion in butter until tender. Combine with remaining ingredients.
10 cups stuffing; enough for one 8- to 10-pound turkey
November 12, 1977

Sesame Seed Stuffing

¾ cup onion, chopped
1 cup celery, chopped
1 cup butter
1 cup sesame seeds, toasted
⅓ cup dried parsley flakes
3 quarts bread cubes, toasted
3 tsp. salt
3 tsp. poultry seasoning
¾ tsp. pepper
¾ cup water or turkey stock

Saute onion and celery in butter. Place sesame seeds in large shallow pan; toast in 350 degree oven for about 20 minutes. Add sesame seeds and other ingredients to onion and celery mixture.
Stuffing for one 12- to 15-pound turkey
November 11, 1967

Peanut Stuffing for Turkey

3-pints peanuts
1 tsp. salt
pinch of cayenne pepper
2 T. butter
1 cup cracker crumbs
1 cup mushrooms, chopped

Scald peanuts and remove the skins; boil them for half an hour then mash fine. Add salt, cayenne, and butter. Then add crumbs and mushrooms.

The mushrooms may be omitted, and two cups of cracker crumbs added, slightly moistened.
May 15, 1908

Chestnut Stuffing

1½ cups onion, finely chopped
1½ cups celery, finely chopped
⅓ cup butter
8 cups dry bread cubes
½ tsp. poultry seasoning
½ tsp. sage
1½ tsp. salt
⅛ tsp. pepper
¼ cup water
1 egg, well beaten
1 cup cooked chestnuts, chopped

Cook onion and celery in butter in a skillet until tender. Add mixture to bread cubes in large pan. Sprinkle with seasonings which have been mixed together and mix well. Add water and egg; toss together with forks. Add chestnuts to mixture and combine.
Stuffing for one 12-pound turkey
November 17, 1956

Vegetable-Walnut Stuffing

⅔ cup butter
2 cups celery, finely chopped
⅔ cup onion, finely chopped
½ cup green pepper, finely chopped
1 tsp. salt
1 tsp. sage
¼ cup water
8 cups dry bread cubes
1 cup walnuts, chopped

Melt butter in skillet. Add celery, onion and green pepper; heat until vegetables become soft, about 10 minutes. Add salt, sage, and water. Combine bread and nuts in large bowl; pour vegetable mixture over bread and nuts; toss lightly to mix ingredients.
Stuffing for one 12- to 16-pound turkey
November 21, 1964

Fruit Stuffing

Basic Recipe
6 cups day-old white bread cubes
(½ inch)
1 tsp. salt
⅓ cup butter
⅓ cup onion, finely minced
½ cup celery, chopped
liquid as needed (½-¾ cup)

Combine all ingredients and fluff with 2 forks until moist.

Variations

To the basic recipe, add:

Apple Date Dressing. 1 cup pecans, chopped; 1 lb. pitted dates, chopped; 1 to 2 cups unpared apple, diced; ¼ tsp. ginger; 4 T. dried parsley flakes; moisten with 1 cup apple juice.

Green Grape Stuffing. 1 tsp. sage; ½ tsp. pepper; 2 cups green seedless grapes.

Cranberry Bread Stuffing. 1½ cups fresh cranberries, chopped; ½ cup sugar; 1½ cups pineapple tidbits, drained; ¼ tsp. nutmeg.

Apricot-Apple Stuffing for Pheasant.
½ cup Turkish-style dried apricots (pitted and dried whole); 1 cup apple, chopped; moisten with white wine as needed. Also, may substitute 3 cups cornbread stuffing mix for white bread crumbs.

Makes 7- to 10-cups of stuffing, depending upon variation. This is an adequate amount to stuff a 7 to 10 pound bird.

Apricot Stuffing

1 pound dried apricots
6 cups toasted bread cubes
1 cup soda cracker crumbs
¼ cup celery flakes
¼ cup instant minced onion
2 T. parsley flakes
1 tsp. marjoram leaves
1 tsp. salt
½ tsp. pepper
⅓ cup butter, melted

Wash apricots and cook according to package directions. Drain and chop fine. Combine with remaining ingredients; toss lightly.
Stuffing for one 8- to 10-pound turkey
November 21, 1964

Prune and Apple Stuffing for Chicken or Goose

3 cups bread cubes
1 cup apples, pared, diced and
    stewed
½ cup prunes, cooked
½ cup nuts, chopped
¼ cup butter, melted
1 tsp. salt
⅛ tsp. pepper

Mix ingredients together, lightly but thoroughly.
Stuffing for one chicken or goose
November 15, 1941

Orange Stuffing for Chicken or Duck

3 cups dry bread cubes
1 cup apple, diced
2-3 cups orange juice
½ cup seedless raisins
4 T. butter, melted
4 T. sugar
salt and pepper

Mix ingredients together, lightly but thoroughly. If additional moisture is needed, add a little hot water.
Stuffing for one chicken or duck
November 15, 1941

Potato Apple Stuffing

⅓ cup butter
1 cup celery, chopped
½ cup onion, chopped
1½ quarts soft bread cubes
1 cup uncooked potato, chopped
1 cup tart apple, chopped
1 tsp. salt
1 tsp. poultry seasoning
⅛ tsp. pepper

Melt butter in skillet; add celery and onion; saute until tender. Combine with bread cubes, potato, apple, salt, poultry seasoning, and pepper. Place in oiled covered 1½-quart casserole.
    Bake in 350 degree oven for 30 minutes.
7 cups stuffing
November 11, 1967

Raisin Bread Stuffing

1 15-ounce loaf sliced raisin bread
1 pound pork sausage
1 cup onion, chopped
1 cup celery, chopped
⅓ cup seedless raisins
1 tsp. thyme
1½ tsp. salt
¼ tsp. pepper

Toast bread and cut into small cubes. Brown sausage, stirring occasionally to break up meat. Drain off and reserve drippings. Combine sausage with bread. Saute onion, celery, and raisins in one-half cup drippings. If less than this amount remains, add butter to make one-half cup. Add thyme, salt, and pepper. Mix lightly with bread and sausage.
Stuffing for 15- to 18-pound turkey
November 15, 1969

Prune Stuffing for Duck

*2 cups soft bread crumbs, pulled
    apart into small pieces*
*½ cup cooked prunes, finely
    chopped*
*1 cup English walnut meats,
    chopped*
2 T. butter, melted
1 T. onion, finely chopped
salt and pepper, to taste
boiling water, as needed

Toss together crumbs, prunes, walnuts, butter, onion, salt, and pepper. Mix so that the butter will be well mixed through the dressing. Add enough boiling water to make a rather moist dressing.
Stuffing for one duck
November 15, 1923

Potato and Walnut Stuffing for Goose or Duck

*3 cups cooked mashed potatoes
    (fresh)*
1 onion, grated
¾ cup walnut meats, chopped
1½ tsp. salt
1 T. butter
1 cup milk
1 egg, beaten
pepper, to taste

Mix all ingredients in the order given. Use right away.
Stuffing for one goose or duck
November 15, 1923

Peanut Stuffing for Duck

2 cups whole wheat bread crumbs
1 cup peanuts, chopped
salt and pepper, to taste
paprika, as desired
3 T. softened peanut butter
½ tsp. onion juice
hot cream, as needed

Mix all ingredients in the order given. Use enough cream to moisten.
Stuffing for one duck
November 15, 1923

Elegant Oyster-Rice Stuffing

1 cup uncooked white rice
2 cups water
2 tsp. salt
3 T. butter
½ cup onion, chopped
¼ tsp. pepper
1 cup celery, chopped
½ pint oysters, chopped
¼ cup water or turkey broth

Put the rice, water, and salt in two-quart saucepan. Bring to a vigorous boil and turn heat as low as possible. Cover pan and leave over low heat for 15 minutes; remove from heat, leaving covered for 10 minutes more. Melt butter. Add onion and celery and cook over medium heat until tender, keeping covered and stirring occasionally. Stir in pepper and add to rice. Add oysters and water or broth and mix gently.
4½ cups stuffing, enough for a small turkey
November 17, 1956

Herbed Liver Stuffing

⅓ cup instant minced onion
⅓ cup celery flakes
⅔ cup water
⅔ cup butter
½ pound beef or lamb liver
½ cup hot water
2 T. parsley flakes
2½ tsp. salt
2 tsp. marjoram leaves
½ tsp. pepper
2 quarts toasted bread cubes

Combine onion, celery flakes, and water. Let stand five minutes to soften; saute in one-quarter cup butter. Add remaining butter. Cook liver in a cup of hot water in a covered saucepan until tender, five to 10 minutes over moderate heat. Put liver through food chopper, using fine blade. Combine with sauted onion, celery, liver water, and remaining ingredients.

Stuffing for one 10- to 12-pound turkey
November 21, 1964

Sweet Potato Sausage Stuffing

2 cups cooked sweet potatoes,
  mashed
6 cups bread cubes, toasted
1 cup celery, chopped
⅔ cup onion, chopped
8 sausage links, cut into 1-inch
  pieces
2½ tsp. salt
½ tsp. pepper
2 T. poultry seasoning
¼ cup butter, melted

Combine sweet potatoes, bread cubes, celery, and onion. Brown sausage; add to the sweet potato mixture. Add seasonings and melted butter. Mix well and spoon lightly into bird cavity.
Stuffing for one 10- to 12-pound turkey
November 21, 1959

Rice-Shrimp Stuffing for Turkey

1 cup green pepper, chopped
1 cup onion, chopped
2 medium cloves garlic, minced
1 tsp. oregano, crushed
2 T. butter or margarine
3 cups cooked rice
1½ cups cooked shrimp, chopped
2 T. pimiento, chopped
½ tsp. salt
2 cans (10½-ounces each) chicken
  giblet gravy

In saucepan cook pepper, onion, and garlic with oregano in butter until tender. Add rice, shrimp, pimiento, salt, and ½ cup of the gravy.*
  *Use remaining gravy to thicken pan drippings after turkey is roasted.
Stuffing for one 10-pound turkey
November 20, 1971

Easy Mincemeat Stuffing

1 quart soft ½-inch bread cubes
¾ cup mincemeat
¼ tsp. salt
dash pepper
¼ cup butter, melted

Toast bread cubes until slightly crisp. Add mincemeat, salt, pepper, and butter. Toss lightly with two forks until well blended.
1 quart stuffing
November 21, 1959

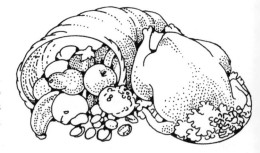

About the Author

Harvard graduate and rice grower Mitzi Ayala of Davis, California, enjoys talking to the non-farm public about agriculture. She does this as the hostess and producer of "Mitzi's Country Magazine," a weekly television program, and as a professional public speaker who gives more than forty-five talks a year. In addition, as a columnist for Capitol News Service, she's the author of more than three hundred seventy-five syndicated newspaper articles. Besides the Prairie Farmer Cookbooks, she is the author of *The Farmer's Cookbook* and *Managerial Innovation.*

Index

Menus

Pheasant Recipes

Relish and Garnishes

Rice

Turkey Recipes

Vegetables